50 Nifty

Activities

for

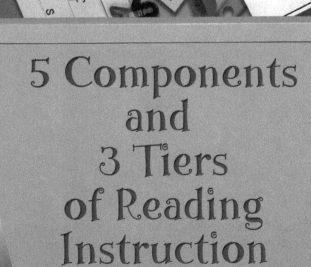

5 Components and 3 Tiers of Reading Instruction

━━━ ◎ ━━━

Judith Dodson

LETRS

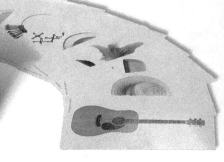

Sopris West®
EDUCATIONAL SERVICES

A Cambium Learning® Company

LONGMONT, CO

ISBN-13: 978-1-60218-205-9
ISBN-10: 1-60218-205-1

Printed in the United States of America
Published and Distributed by

Sopris West®
EDUCATIONAL SERVICES

A Cambium Learning® Company

17855 Dallas Pkwy, Suite 400 • Dallas, Texas 75287
(800) 547-6747 • www.voyagersopris.com

᭝᭝᭝ **Dedication** ᭝᭝᭝

This book is dedicated to some special people in my life.

To my parents: My mother, who taught me to love reading, and my father, who taught me to love to dance. I believe this translated into my passion for teaching children to read and enhanced my direct instruction with movement—of letters, words, or bodies—as much as possible!

To Louisa Moats: You were my mentor from afar, years before I met you. I had read and studied your ideas and let them guide my development and work as a teacher. Then, you inspired me to share your brilliant work with other teachers, empowering them with knowledge they are hungry for. I continue to learn from you through your grace, dignity, passion, and friendship. I am honored by your faith in me.

To the national *Language Essentials for Teachers of Reading and Spelling* (LETRS) trainers: Your passion and commitment inspire and teach me. Carol, you are a special friend—always there to teach, share, support, and cheer me on. Thank you.

To my Colorado Reading friends: You have supported my thinking and practice around teaching reading for over a decade. We are a loving friendship and work group, and I am grateful to each of you for your help and hugs over the years.

To the children who have graced my life with the opportunity and joy of teaching you to read: You taught me that I needed to change my goal from teaching you to read to teaching you to love the process of learning to read. You ignited a passion in me that warms and inspires me still, even though I am no longer with you each day. You remain in my heart always.

To my family: You are my heart. I thank you for giving me the love and sanctuary of the life we have together. I am blessed with your support, faith, and confidence in me. From sleepless nights and too-early mornings as I worried about my students when I was in the classroom, to trips to the airport now to put me on a plane to teach teachers in some other part of the country, you are always there, saying "yes" and blessing me with your love. Thank you Rocco, Noah, Danny, and Ana. You are at the very heart of me, and you are at the heart of my work.

About the Author

Judi Dodson, M.A., is a national LETRS trainer, who works with teachers and administrators of primary, intermediate, and secondary students. She served for 20 years as a special education teacher, primarily with children with reading problems, and as an educational consultant performing diagnostic assessment of learning disabilities. Judi is currently working on writing activities that can help classroom teachers develop and enhance their students' oral language skills.

Judi consults with schools, state departments of education, and school districts on issues related to school change, teacher knowledge, and literacy achievement. She speaks at conferences and gives workshops on topics related to reading intervention and activities that support increasing student achievement. Judi believes that working to empower teachers with knowledge about literacy can make a real difference in their work and help them change and enrich the lives of the children they teach.

Judi lives in the Rocky Mountains of Colorado with her husband and daughter and has two grown sons. She divides her time between her family, writing, teaching teachers, and as president of Peruvian Hearts, a nonprofit organization that supports education, healthcare, and nutritional needs of children living in orphanages in Peru.

Contents

Foreword ix

Preface xi

Introduction 1

Phonemic Awareness Activities 7

    Sound Toss 9

    Tap It, Map It, and Zap It 12

    Star Sounds 15

    Listen and Clap 18

    Rhyming Rhythms 20

    Walkabout Sound Matching 23

    Concept Maps 25

    Faces of Our Friends 28

    Clothespin Sounds 30

    Flyswatter Sounds 33

Phonics Activities 37

    Tap It, Map It, and Graph It 39

    Physical Phonics 42

    I'm Magic e 45

    Language Links 48

    Picture Perfect Spelling 51

    Syllable Tracking 54

    Clothespin Phonics 57

    Where Is the Sound? 60

    Flip Over Sounds 62

    Walkabout Words 65

Fluency Activities 67

    Phrase Reading 70

    Reading Buddies 73

    Alphabetic Prosody 75

    Read With Speed 77

    Triplet Reading 80

    Ready, Set, Say It 83

    Wear a Word 86

    Words by Heart 88

    Flyswatter Syllables 91

    Schoolwide Reading 94

Vocabulary Activities 97

    Making Words My Own 100

    How Well Do I Know It? 103

    Flyswatter Morphemes 106

    Bringing Words to Scale 108

    Word Webs 111

    A Special Word 114

    Sports Card Words 117

    Word Train 119

    Branching Out 121

    Schoolwide Vocabulary 123

Comprehension Activities 127

    Picture Perfect Notes 130

    Links to My Life 133

    Coding for Concepts 135

    Thinking in Pictures 138

    The Comprehension Train 141

    Growing Sentences 144

    What's in the Bucket? 146

    Sentence Mix-Ups 149

    Picturing the Story 152

    Living Concept Maps 155

Appendix A: Worksheets 159

Appendix B: Letter Cards 191

Bibliography 205

Glossary 207

Foreword

When I first saw the proofs of this book, I could barely contain my delight! The activities are fun, practical, and authentic. If I were still teaching children, I'd want this at my elbow. Judi Dodson is a master of her craft. Not only does she comprehend deeply the rationale for all of these instructional activities in reading, but she herself implements them with consummate skill. The activities she has selected to address the five essential components of research-based reading instruction are ones she has used with students of all ability levels. The adaptations for whole class, small group, and intensive needs students reflect Judi's exceptional knowledge of individual differences.

Judi has put together a perfect companion piece to LETRS. Here in one charming volume are 50 "things to do on Monday morning" that are consistent with the science of reading. Most importantly, Judi has graced this book with her wit, charm, and love of children. It's infectious. Enjoy!

—Louisa Moats

ᘰᘾᘰ Preface ᘰᘾᘰ

Twenty-one years ago I sat in a classroom in the Rocky Mountains of Colorado and taught my first student to read. Cody had been referred to me by his first grade teacher, who was feeling frustrated because she had not been able to teach him to read. As a young special education teacher, I knew in my heart that I really didn't know how to teach him to read either. My teacher training had included classes in children's literature but not reading methods. I felt the weight of the responsibility of the task that I was being asked to do.

I looked in the reading closet at my school, which held a lot of old materials, searching for ideas. I found some alphabet letter cards and simple texts. We started with sounds and letters, systematically and sequentially, because I didn't have any other ideas. When Cody knew enough of the sounds and letters to begin decoding words, we began using some of the simple texts I had found in the reading closet. As Cody began to read of the adventures of Matt and Tab, I found myself crying. Somehow, even as a young and very naïve teacher, I knew that what had just happened was life changing for Cody. What I didn't realize was that it was life changing for me, too. I didn't know that in that moment my love of teaching children to read had been born, and I would spend the rest of my professional life trying to learn as much as I could about the art and science of teaching reading. I couldn't anticipate then that after my 20 years in the classroom I would transfer that passion to teaching other teachers what I had learned about sharing the gift of reading with students.

Teaching children to read can change the trajectory of their lives! It opens doors that might have been closed to them. Yet for many children those doors remain shut. They struggle with learning to read and fall behind their peers in reading skills, with the gap growing each year they are in school. These children need more opportunities to practice specific skills in order to achieve mastery before they go on to the next skill. Often, however, the class is moving faster than some students are moving, and meaningful opportunities for practice may be limited.

The activities in this book provide engaging and enjoyable ways for children to get the practice they need while helping them discover that reading can be fun. For many years as teachers we were told that "drill makes kill!" If we give students drill in the basic skills of reading, they will lose their motivation to read. I would like to frame this concept of practice differently. I believe that "drill makes skill." I would challenge you to think of anything you are good at—sports, music, sewing, knitting. Have you gotten to be good at that activity without lots of practice? Did you find that the practice increases your skills and thereby increases your motivation for doing that activity? The same holds true for reading. When we give children enough opportunities to practice their skills so that those skills become mastered and automatic, we then find their motivation also increases. Practice does not kill their motivation, it improves it; children are motivated to do those things they feel skilled at. Our children will not become lifelong readers, which is the goal of every teacher, without the skills that make reading easy and pleasurable.

50 Nifty Activities for 5 Components and 3 Tiers of Reading Instruction is designed for teachers who are using a comprehensive approach to reading instruction that includes the five essential components of reading: phonemic awareness, phonics, fluency, vocabulary, and comprehension (National Reading Panel, 2000). The book was developed as a supplement to the *Language Essentials for Teachers of Reading and Spelling* (LETRS) (Moats, 2005) curriculum. It is based on the concept that professional development in evidence-based reading research and the foundations of reading is critical to fostering reading achievement in all students. With the increasing awareness of the effectiveness of data-driven instruction, the activities in this book have been aligned to *Dynamic Indicators of Basic Early Literacy Skills* (DIBELS) (Good & Kaminski, 2003) and can be easily aligned to other instruments used to assess and monitor the five components of reading. Additionally, there are accommodations and suggestions for English language learners (ELLs) and ideas for extending activities to more advanced learners.

I hope that *50 Nifty Activities* will help give your students meaningful and enjoyable ways to practice the skills in which they need extra help. As a reading teacher you have the power to change the lives of your students. Your time with them is precious, and it is my greatest hope that this book of simple but effective activities will help enhance your ability to make a positive impact on their reading achievement and their lives.

∿∿∿ **Introduction** ∿∿∿

50 Nifty Activities for 5 Components and 3 Tiers of Reading Instruction provides a multisensory, lively, and engaging approach to literacy instruction. The activities in this book reinforce some of the most important concepts of literacy instruction that have been validated through evidence-based research in literacy development. The activities are grounded in phonemic awareness, phonics, fluency, vocabulary, and comprehension—the five components of reading that have been determined to be the essential components of any comprehensive reading program (National Reading Panel, 2000). The book is divided into five sections, one for each reading component. In addition, each activity includes three variations designed to support teaching at one of the three tiers of instruction—whole class (the universal level), small group (for strategic and intensive needs students), and independent or paired (for strategic and intensive needs students who need extra reinforcement and practice). These levels, or tiers, of instruction are meant to help the classroom teacher differentiate teaching based on the learning needs of all students in the classroom.

Instructional Practices

The activities in this book are taught in a systematic and sequential format and are crafted to enhance your ability to connect essential foundational knowledge and the application of that knowledge in the classroom. For example, activities that enhance reading comprehension also emphasize the link between oral language and reading comprehension. We know that if children don't understand something at the oral level, they will be less likely to understand it at the text level. Therefore, going back to the oral level gives us greater efficacy at the text level. Activities showing an icon that denotes "The Talking Classroom" connect oral language development to the targeted skill.

Managing Flexible Grouping

Each activity has three variations: whole classroom instruction, small group work, and independent practice. This differentiated instruction is based on the original skill and its purpose. Each variation enables students to remain engaged in the learning process. First, students are introduced to a skill in a whole class setting; next, students work in small, flexible groupings; and finally they practice the skill on their own and/or with a partner. Each activity allows for a gradual release of responsibility from teacher modeling to guided practice and ultimately to independent practice for students.

Establishing Routines

You will recognize similar activities as you work your way through the five sections of this book. For example, you will see an activity called Flyswatter Sounds in the Phonemic Awareness section. This activity can be used to build automaticity at the sound as well as at the word level. It also reappears as Flyswatter Morphemes, an activity for the development and reinforcement of morphological knowledge in the Vocabulary section, and then again as Flyswatter Syllables, a means of enhancing students' ability to recognize and practice orthographic patterns, leading to greater automaticity for reading big words. As you get comfortable with the activity and the concept behind it, as well as the ease with which it can be incorporated into the classroom, you will see that it can be easily be adapted for use with any concept you have already directly taught and want to work with for increased automaticity and fluency.

By having a range of extremely flexible activities, both you and your students will develop a deep understanding of why they are being used and how to use them. The flexibility will add novelty to the reinforcement and practice while the familiarity will strengthen routines that are important for learning and student success. The repetition of design in the activities will build ownership on your part and confidence in your ability to use the activity successfully. Instructional routines add comfort and efficacy for both teachers and students.

Sharing the Purpose of the Activity

When students understand how the skills they are learning will help them become better readers, they are more likely to retain, recall, and apply what they are learning, thus helping them become more skillful and motivated readers. The activities in this book have been designed to give students enough practice so that they deepen their understanding and mastery of key reading concepts. Each activity explains the purpose of the lesson and returns to the purpose later on. Sharing the purpose with your students helps them understand why they are doing each activity.

Building Word Consciousness/Creating Language Detectives

Word consciousness refers to students' awareness of words in their environment beyond the instructional setting. When students are word conscious, they are looking for words, listening for words, watching for words, and using words.

Word consciousness starts at the sound level. It goes next to orthography, as students look for patterns in their reading and in the world around them. It continues with vocabulary and comprehension, with students looking for information and words related to themes and topics about which they have been reading and studying. Word learning and word discovery, with positive reinforcement, can be exciting for students. The activities in this book lend themselves to developing word consciousness in students.

An important way that you can help develop word consciousness is by reinforcing word finding. This can be done by issuing stickers, points, or food; by letting students ring a bell, tell the class, or put a star on a chart; or by granting students computer time. One idea to reinforce word finding is to make a picture of a detective with a big magnifying glass (or use a real one). Perhaps you could get little magnifying glasses for the whole class and take a picture of everyone as they begin their careers as language detectives! You could then call your living word wall "Language Detectives Cracking the Code!"

Positively reinforcing word learning helps children enjoy the process. Therefore, setting up a system of reinforcement for discovery will get your class excited to learn about and find words. Get ready to have fun with your students as you work together to crack the code of the English language and share a love of reading and literacy learning.

Instructional Tips

The following guidelines will help you effectively choose and plan the activities in this book.

1. **Base your instructional choices on assessment results.** Continue to monitor students' progress in order to judge the efficacy of your instruction.

2. **Plan an I Do, We Do, You Do** format, where appropriate. Modeling, guiding practice with feedback, and then releasing the students for independent practice will set the stage for successful learning. Remember that practice does not make perfect; only perfect practice (guided with feedback when necessary) makes perfect.

3. **Create opportunities for frequent, distributed practice**. Frequent, distributed practice is more effective for retention and recall of information than longer, less frequent learning sessions.

4. **Link prior learning to the new learning.** Making these connections for students will increase their understanding and retention of the new information.

5. **Include multisensory aspects of the activities.** The use of multisensory approaches can increase attention, engagement, and retention of information.

6. **Include opportunities for oral language to develop.** "The Talking Classroom" suggestions embedded throughout the activities will give students practice in talking, listening, responding, and elaborating.

7. **Give students opportunities to create their own mental images.** Creating mental images helps deepen the meaning of new words and concepts. It also creates a personal connection to the learning and enhances the retention and retrieval of information.

8. **Incorporate humor into your lessons.** Humor can increase students' attention, motivation, and sense of connection to the learning, which can enhance retention and retrieval of information.

9. **Bundle skills and strategies to maximize opportunities for distributed practice.** Once students have learned a strategy, the strategy can be applied to new learning. For example, when studying a new word, the students can name the sounds and syllables, define the word, and use the word in a sentence.

10. **Modify your instruction if progress monitoring does not show adequate growth.** Progress monitoring is only effective if it drives your instruction. Check regularly for growth in skills and understanding. If you do not see sufficient growth in your students, consider changing the amount of instruction time, the focus of the instruction, and the group size and makeup.

11. **Accelerate as well as remediate.** Let progress monitoring guide your instructional decisions. When learning has been successful, move quickly to the next concept to close the achievement gap.

12. **Connect with your students at their hearts.** Providing eye contact and authentic conversation, as well as linking learning to students' cultural backgrounds and experience, can make the classroom environment more likely to foster engagement and motivation, leading to new learning and greater achievement.

The Reading Brain

Oral language lays the foundation for literacy learning. For centuries, the human brain has been hardwired for speech and understanding oral language. However, learning a written code is a relatively new task for the human brain. While oral language is a naturally occurring skill, reading is a skill that, for most people, must be systematically and explicitly taught.

Since the 1980s, advances in brain imaging have given reading researchers the ability to study the brain during the act of reading. This ability has led to a deeper understanding of what is happening in students' brains as they read. We now know that four areas of the brain are involved in reading:

◎ The **occipital lobes,** located at the back of the brain, are responsible for receiving and interpreting visual input.

◎ The **parietal lobes** are located above the occipital lobes and are responsible for taking in tactile information and for the integration of stimuli related to sound and sight.

◎ On the sides of the brain are the **temporal lobes,** responsible for taking in and interpreting auditory stimuli.

◎ The **frontal lobes** are located toward the front of the brain. They are responsible for thinking about language—making the connections.

The Four Processing Systems of the Brain

The four processing systems are the neurological systems that support the reading process. This model, originally created by Seidenberg and McClellan, is discussed at length in Marilyn Adams' book, *Beginning to Read: Learning and Thinking about Print*. Because of the multiple systems involved in the reading process, the roots of reading problems may originate in any or all of the processing systems.

The Phonological Processor processes the speech sound system. This system is involved in:

- Identifying, comparing, and manipulating sounds
- Pronouncing and producing sounds and words
- Memorizing sounds, words, and phrases
- Linking sounds, spellings, and meanings

The Orthographic Processor processes letters, letter patterns, and whole words. This system helps us:

- Recognize and form letters
- Associate letters with speech sounds
- Recognize letter sequences and patterns
- Recognize whole words
- Recall letters for spelling

The Meaning Processor stores word meanings. These include:

- Other words in same semantic field
- Categories and concepts
- Examples of words in phrase context
- Sounds, spellings, and syllables in words
- Meaningful parts (mor-phemes) of words

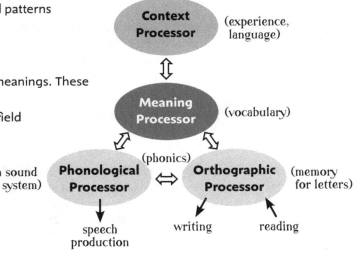

The Context Processor inteprets words we have heard in relationship to:

- Experience
- Background knowledge of the concepts involved
- Multiple meanings of words
- Sentence structure and sequences

English Language Learners

The activities in this book can easily be adapted for students who are learning English as a second language. Each activity includes simple suggestions for doing so. The activities can also be modified for use in a second language for those children being taught in their native language.

Oral language development is a critical foundation element for all literacy learning. Weaving oral language opportunities into all literacy learning activities will increase the opportunities for students to practice their newly developing language skills. It takes many opportunities for practice over time for students to develop the skills they need to read, write, and think in their new language.

Here are some general guidelines to help your English language learners (ELLs) succeed:

- Seat students close to where you will be instructing so that they can get more clues for understanding as well as feedback from you. Seating these students near you will help them stay engaged with the lesson, even though their language is limited.

- When appropriate, give the students a preview of the lesson to be taught before presenting it to the whole class.

- Emphasize a multisensory approach to the activities.

- Emphasize oral language development throughout the instructional day for all ELL students in the classroom.

- Read and reread simple texts aloud, in English and in the students' native language when possible, to give students the opportunity to be exposed to good oral language models.

- Use texts that are repetitive and contain rhythmic patterns. Texts should be simple and culturally sensitive. Use clear, short sentences during classroom instruction and discussion, being sure to increase the complexity and sophistication of language as the students' oral language skills develop.

- Accept approximations of words, reinforcing all attempts at oral language. Understand differences of the sounds of the native language and the sounds needed for success in English.

- Give increased "wait time" for children to think about and formulate responses.

- Use music and rhythmic activities to enhance oral language engagement and learning.

- Use familiar pictures and objects to enhance oral language practice with the known. Use pictures and objects of new words and concepts to enhance language learning.

- Have students rehearse orally to help them formulate oral language that can then be transferred into writing. Begin writing with structured activities that support the transference of oral sentence formulation to the written form. Support writing with pictures.

- Provide opportunities for modeling, guided feedback, and frequent distributed paired practice to reinforce language learning. Increase the amount of modeling in the I Do, We Do, You Do model.

- Encourage cooperative learning (peer interaction), which increases risk taking in terms of oral expression because students are part of a group and the group can support their efforts with language.

Dig In to Learn More

Adams, M. (1990). *Beginning to read: Learning and thinking about print.* Cambridge, MA: MIT Press.

Moats, L. C. (2005). *LETRS Module 1: The challenge of learning to read.* Longmont, CO: Sopris West Educational Services.

National Reading Panel. (2000). *Teaching children to read: An evidence-based assessment of the scientific research on reading and its implications for reading instruction.* Washington, DC: U.S. Government Printing Office.

Shaywitz, S. E. (2003). *Overcoming dyslexia: A new and complete science-based program for reading problems at any level.* New York: Alfred A. Knopf.

Snow, C. E., Burns, M. S., & Griffin, P. (1998). *Preventing reading difficulties in young children.* Washington, DC: National Academy Press.

Wolfe, P., & Nevills, P. (2004). *Building the reading brain.* Thousand Oaks, CA: Corwin Press.

Phonemic Awareness ⌣·⌣·⌣ Activities ⌣·⌣·⌣

1. Sound Toss
2. Tap It, Map It, and Zap It
3. Star Sounds
4. Listen and Clap
5. Rhyming Rhythms
6. Walkabout Sound Matching
7. Concept Maps
8. Faces of Our Friends
9. Clothespin Sounds
10. Flyswatter Sounds

Phonemic awareness refers to the ability to be sensitive to the speech sounds of the English language. The skills involved include hearing, identifying, segmenting, blending, and manipulating individual sounds (phonemes) within spoken words. Phonemic awareness is only one part of the overarching umbrella of phonological processing. Phonological processing refers to various aspects of speech and language perception, such as interpreting, storing, and retrieving information. Skills under the larger phonological umbrella include the ability to recognize how many words are in a sentence and the number of syllables in a word, as well as the ability to recognize and produce words that rhyme, and ultimately to perceive phonemes within words. Phonological skills can be observed in how an individual learns a foreign language, recalls names and facts, and sounds out words for spelling.

Phonemic awareness is considered one of the best early predictors of school success (National Reading Panel, 2000). More than 50 studies have demonstrated the importance of phonemic awareness instruction in preventing and treating reading problems.

Explicit instruction in phonemic awareness skills increases students' ability to hear the discrete sounds in words for greater ease with reading and spelling. Phonemic awareness gives students the foundation they need to make phonics instruction more meaningful and effective by fostering a deeper understanding of the sound/symbol connections that are at the heart of an alphabetic system. The activities in this section will reinforce some of the key phonological processing skills that are closely related to reading and spelling skills.

The Four Processing Systems Connection

The simple activities in this section engage the phonological processor first. However, the meaning processor and the context processor also come into play. The more students know about a word being used for phonemic awareness instruction, the easier it will be for them to learn, recall, and apply the word knowledge. You can reinforce the oral activities in this section by having students identify and write the grapheme (letter sound) with which the word starts. This reinforcement will develop the sound/symbol connection and will engage the orthographic processor in the task. When all four processors are engaged, the learning is deepened.

The LETRS Connection

◎ *Language Essentials for Teachers of Reading and Spelling* (LETRS), Module 2—*The Speech Sounds of English: Phonetics, Phonology, and Phoneme Awareness.*

The Assessment Connection

◎ *DIBELS: Dynamic Indicators of Basic Early Literacy Skills.* Initial Sound Fluency: Assesses level of automaticity of initial sound recognition and production.

◎ *DIBELS: Dynamic Indicators of Basic Early Literacy Skills.* Phoneme Segmentation Fluency: Assesses level of automaticity with hearing and segmenting sounds within spoken words.

The ELL Connection

Many of the activities in this section will be effective with ELLs without any alteration. However, a few small changes can have a great impact on the achievement and skill development for these students. The following are a few ideas to try that may enhance the effectiveness of the phonemic awareness activities:

◎ It is easier for second language learners to process a word phonologically when they can attach meaning to the word.

  ℰ Add objects or pictures to augment a word presented orally. For example, say, "What is the first sound in *star*?" Show a picture of a star, or have a star sticker or object for students to hold.

  ℰ Have students echo words that are presented orally so they can practice the pronunciation and get more repetitions of the word. This will enhance students' ability to develop familiarity with the word and retain, retrieve, and use it correctly.

  ℰ Using gestures can help to engage the new ELL student with the meaning of the word and help to make the task more meaningful.

◎ When working with a word for phonemic awareness skill development, enhance the activity using each word in a short, simple sentence to deepen connections for vocabulary development and comprehension skills.

◎ Many phonemic awareness activities can be done using words in the student's first language.

◎ In Spanish, phonemic awareness activities can be done at the syllable level. For example, instead of asking for "gato" to be counted by sound, /g/ /a/ /t/ /o/, consider asking for it to be counted by syllable, /ga/ /to/.

◎ Sound boxes can be used as syllable boxes.

◎ Using high utility words will address vocabulary and phonemic awareness achievement at the same time.

Dig In to Learn More

Adams, M. J. (1990). *Beginning to read: Learning and thinking about print.* Cambridge, MA: MIT Press.

Good, R. H. III, & Kaminski, R. (2003). *DIBELS: Dynamic indicators of basic early literacy skills.* Longmont, CO: Sopris West Educational Services.

Moats, L. C. (2000). *Speech to print: Language essentials for teachers.* Baltimore, MD: Paul H. Brookes Publishing.

National Reading Panel. (2000). *Report of the National Reading Panel: Teaching children to read: An evidence-based assessment of the scientific research literature on reading and its implications for reading instruction.* Washington, DC: U.S. Government Printing Office.

Sound Toss

Activity Overview

The ability to segment and blend sounds within words is a critical phonemic awareness skill and appears to be the core deficit in students who have weak phonemic awareness. Sound Toss is an activity that develops and reinforces skills in phonemic segmentation and blending. By helping students hear, identify, and use sounds, Sound Toss promotes their achievement in reading, writing, and spelling.

Materials . . . .

- Timer
- Koosh ball* or other ball or object (to toss)
- Sound Toss Worksheet (see Appendix A)
- Picture cards (or objects)
- Dice
- Slinkys*

* Available in the optional Classroom Manipulatives Kit

Whole Classroom Instruction

Set the purpose. Say: "Good readers and spellers can listen to and hear sounds in words easily. Sound Toss will give you practice in listening for sounds in words, making it easier for you to hear, identify, and use sounds."

1. Before you begin this activity, have the class stand in a circle. Start with a game that reinforces attention and listening, such as Silent Ball. For phonemic awareness instruction to be effective, students who have difficulty hearing sounds need to have a quiet environment in which to listen and learn. Silent Ball is a fun way in which to give students the experience of silence and help them understand the value of silence for listening and learning.

   - Explain that all students must be silent. If anyone makes a noise or giggles, the game will end.

   - Have students toss the Koosh ball randomly to one another, remaining silent while the ball is tossed and caught.

   - Keep time for the group to see how long they are able to stay silent. Have the group work against itself in future timings to see if they can increase their ability to stay silent.

2. Sound Toss: Consult the "Scope and Sequence of Skills" to guide instruction. Decide on a level and choose the game.

   - Sound Toss can be played with the whole class at first and later using several small groups at the same time.

   - For fluency practice, you can time the groups to help them increase the speed with which they can generate words.

- Choose one student to be a "counter" in each group. That person counts the number of words stated during the game (for example, 12 rhyming words in a minute). Groups can then play against each other or against themselves, trying to increase the number that they have achieved.

- While students can use real or make-believe words, make sure that they say "This is a make-believe word" when they use one. Later in the day, this will help you to address vocabulary that might come up during the activity. Keep track of words that might not be familiar to your whole class.

Return to the purpose. Say: "You've been practicing listening to different sounds in words. Good readers and spellers can hear different sounds easily. Sound Toss will make it easier for you to hear, identify, and use sounds."

Small Group Work

1. You control the ball now. Toss the ball to everyone in the group individually. In doing this, you can individualize your questions based on the needs of the students:

   - You may toss to the first student and ask, "What is the first sound in *doll*?" The child answers "/d/" and throws the ball back to you.

   - Ask the next student, "What are the sounds in the word *dog*?" The student answers "/d/ /ŏ/ /g/," tapping the sounds to ensure that she has all of the sounds. (For more about tapping sounds, see the next activity, Tap It.)

   - Ask the next student, "If the word is *tap*, can you tell me a word that rhymes with *tap*?"

Talking Classroom

2. Continue the activity for five minutes, allowing each student several opportunities for practice and enough time for you to informally assess the students' skill levels.

Scope and Sequence of Skills

1. **Word-level segmentation:** Students toss the ball saying one word at a time of a poem, song, or rhyme: "Hickory" [toss], "Dickory" [toss], "Dock."

2. **Alliteration:** Students toss the ball saying words that begin with a given sound, for instance, words that start with /t/: "table" [toss], "tap" [toss], "tiger" [toss], "trap" [toss].

3. **Syllable segmentation:** Students toss the ball segmenting a poem, sentence, song, or rhyme at the syllable level: "Hick-" [toss], "or-" [toss], "y" [toss], "Dick-" [toss], "or-" [toss], "y" [toss], "Dock" [toss].

4. **Rhyme production/rhyming time:** Students toss the ball saying words that rhyme with a given word, such as *bat* (words can be real or nonsense words): "bat" [toss], "cat" [toss], "hat" [toss].

5. **Sound segmentation** (Beginning and Ending Sound Game): Toss the ball to a student and say a word, such as *tap*. The student says a word beginning with the last sound of your word, and the next student says a word with the last sound of the prior student's word, and so on: "tap" [toss], "pan" [toss], "knife" [toss], "fork" [toss], "kiss" [toss], "sat" [toss].

3. Talk with your students about the words being used in Sound Toss. Vocabulary development can be incorporated throughout all Sound Toss activities.

Independent Practice

1. Give each student a Sound Toss Worksheet (see Appendix A), picture cards, a die, and a Slinky. Have students choose a picture card.

2. Students will roll the die several times:
   - If they roll a 1, have students write the first sound of the picture on their worksheet. If the picture is of a man, the student writes the letter *m* (for the /m/ sound).
   - If they roll a 2, have students write the second sound: *a*.
   - If they roll a 3, have students write the third sound: *n*.
   - If they roll a 4, have students tap out all the sounds: /m/ /ă/ /n/.
   - If they roll a 5, have students say a rhyming word: *fan*.
   - If they roll a 6, have students pick up the Slinky and say the word slowly as they stretch out the Slinky, then say the word fast as they bring the Slinky back together quickly: "Mmmmmmmaaaaaaaaannnnnnnn, man."

Stretching Students' Learning

- Advanced versions of Sound Toss can be played using multisyllabic words.
- Play the Beginning and Ending Sound Game with students using multisyllabic words.

Tap It, Map It, and Zap It

Activity Overview

The ability to segment and blend sounds within words is critical to phonemic awareness proficiency. Students with weak phonemic awareness show a core deficit in their ability to segment and blend sounds. Tap It, Map It, and Zap It develops and reinforces skills in the area of phonemic segmentation and blending. Phonemic awareness lays down the foundation upon which phonics is built. When students become automatic with their phonemic awareness skills, they will be able to read, write, and spell with greater ease.

Materials

- Sound Box Worksheet (see Appendix A)
- Whiteboard, dry-erase marker, and eraser
- Student whiteboards, dry-erase markers, and erasers
- Pictures
- Magnetic wand and discs* (or items that can be used as markers for sound mapping, such as cereal, counters, paper squares, blocks)

* Available in the optional Classroom Manipulatives Kit

Whole Classroom Instruction

Set the purpose. Say: "This activity will give you practice listening to sounds in words. Being able to hear the different sounds will help you to become great readers, writers, and spellers."

1. Sit in a circle on the floor with the students (or they may be seated at their desks).

2. Consulting the Sound Box Worksheet, make a set of boxes on the whiteboard and ask students to do the same on their whiteboards.

3. Choose a picture.
   - Say the name of the picture.
   - Ask students to repeat the name of the picture with you.

4. Discuss the vocabulary of the picture to build background knowledge and oral language.

5. Model sound tapping. Hold up one hand and demonstrate how to tap out sounds with your fingers; touch the thumb to the index finger, then the middle finger, ring finger, and pinkie.
   - If the picture is of a dog, tap out the sounds with your fingers, /d/ /ŏ/ /g/.

- ℮ End by pulling the sounds together (pull down as you make a fist).
- ℮ You have now segmented and blended the sounds in the target word. Blending is very important to later achievement of reading fluency.

6. Place a set of four or five discs (or markers) at the top of your work space (if you are using an overhead projector, this will work fine).

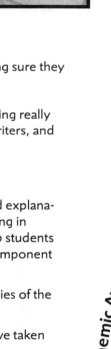

- ℮ Map the sounds in *dog*, /d/ /ŏ/ /g/, using the magnetic discs: Move the discs into the boxes, with each disc representing one of the phonemes in the word *dog*, /d/ /ŏ/ /g/.
- ℮ Put your finger under each marker and touch and say the sounds as you touch each disc.
- ℮ Blend the sounds back together, moving your finger under the boxes and discs and say the word *dog* smoothly as you draw your finger across from left to right.
- ℮ Take the magnetic wand and quickly say the word *dog* again as you "zap" (brush aside) the discs with the wand.

7. Tap, map, and zap a few more words with the students. Make sure to have students do the blending, in addition to the segmentation, with each word.

8. Have students tap, map, and zap a few words independently as you watch, making sure they understand the process.

Return to the purpose. Say: "You have been practicing listening to sounds in words. Being really good at hearing the different sounds in words will help you to become great readers, writers, and spellers."

Small Group Work

Prepare in advance for the sound work to determine which words may be new and need explanation for your students. Select words from text you will be reading in the small group. Bring in pictures or objects to demonstrate the meaning, build background knowledge, and help students create a mental image of the word. This also adds a lively, multisensory oral language component to your phonemic awareness instruction.

1. Distribute magnetic wands and discs to be used with student whiteboards or copies of the Sound Box Worksheet to each student in the group.

2. Have students repeat the Tap It, Map It, and Zap It procedure using words you have taken from text they will read later.

Independent Practice

Tap It, Map It, and Zap It can be repeated with students working in pairs this time.

- ☺ Give each pair of students a bag with objects in it or a stack of pictures. Students may also use a book they have read with their teacher to find words to tap, map, and zap. Ask students to follow the Tap It, Map It, and Zap It procedure and to give each other 5–10 pictures, objects, or words to tap, map, and zap. Students take turns being the "teacher" and the "student."

Phonemic Awareness Tap It, Map It, Zap It

Stretching Students' Learning

- Use increasingly complex words for sound mapping.

- Students can zap the markers one at a time and write the appropriate letters in their place, or leave the markers down on the first row of boxes and write the appropriate grapheme (letter or letters) under the sound marker that it matches.

- Use multisyllabic words with the markers representing the syllables.

Star Sounds

Activity Overview

The ability to listen for and reflect on sounds is the foundation upon which literacy skills are built. Star Sounds is an activity that builds phonemic awareness listening skills by giving students opportunities to listen for, think about, and respond to sounds. It reinforces the ability to make sound/symbol connections, and it stimulates full engagement for students by employing a multisensory learning experience.

Materials • • • • • •

- ◎ Masking tape
- ◎ Star Cards Template (see Appendix A)
- ◎ Objects (or pictures) and small bags to hold them
- ◎ Letter cards (see Appendix B)
- ◎ Plastic hand clappers* (*optional*)
- ◎ Paper with a line down the middle
- ◎ Chart paper and marker
- ◎ Star stickers (or student-generated stars)
- ◎ Star Sounds Worksheet (see Appendix A)

* Available in the optional Classroom Manipulatives Kit

Whole Classroom Instruction

Set the purpose. Say: "You are going to practice listening for sounds in words that I say. You may be listening for a sound at the beginning of a word, at the end of a word, or maybe even in the middle of a word. Being able to hear the different sounds that make up words will make you really good readers, writers, and spellers."

This activity can be done with objects and with words presented orally if the class does not need the extra support of objects and pictures.

1. Create two circles on the floor with tape. Make the circles large enough for half the class to stand inside of each.

2. Give out star cards and hand clappers, if available, to all the students in the class. Use the Star Cards Template to make star cards.

3. Distribute one object to each student. Some of the objects should fit the target sounds of instruction. For example, if the target sounds are initial /p/ and /m/, have an actual pan and a mop that the students can hold.

4. Have one student stand in each circle holding a card with a grapheme that represents one of the target sounds. For example, cards might have the letters *p* and *m,* representing the sounds /p/ and /m/.

5. Give two other students objects that represent the initial target sound for each circle.

6. Say the word *milk*. Ask the class to repeat the word. Hold up an empty container of milk. Say to the class, "I can tap out the sounds in *milk*: milk, /m/ /ĭ/ /l/ /k/. I hear the sound /mmmm/ at the beginning of the word *milk*."

   ℮ Model by taking your star card and moving it into the circle with the student who is holding the *m*.

   ℮ Ask students to clap their hand clappers (or put their thumbs up or clap their hands) if they agree that *milk* starts with /m/ and that you are standing in the correct circle.

These students are working with /p/ *paint* and /m/ *map*.

7. Call on students one at a time. Have students hold up the object you gave them. If a student thinks the beginning sound of her object matches one of the star sounds (target sounds), she can go and stand in the circle with the matching sound. (If students need extra support, you can tap the words together, helping them to reflect on the sound at the beginning of the words.) Have students take hand clappers into the circle so they can continue to clap for other students.

   ℮ If the rest of the students in the class agree, they clap their clappers to show their agreement (or clap their hands or show thumbs up/thumbs down).

   ℮ If the student does not have a matching object, she can then think of a word that starts with one of the star sounds and can stand in the appropriate circle.

Return to the purpose. Say: "You have been practicing listening for sounds in words. Hearing sounds in words will help you read, write, and spell really well."

Small Group Work

1. Use chart paper and star stickers to demonstrate.

2. Distribute the Star Sounds Worksheet and a sheet of star stickers to students. (Have students add extra columns to the worksheet if you think they are ready.)

3. Depending on the sound skill you are targeting, choose an object and a grapheme that matches that sound. It can be a beginning, middle, or ending sound. For example, if the target is the middle sound /ă/ and the middle sound /ĭ/, you could choose a cat and the letter *a* and a toy pig and the letter *i*.

4. Using a whiteboard, model the process once or twice. Say a word that represents one of the target sounds: "*Map*: I can tap it out. I hear an /ă/ sound in the middle of *map*, so I will put a star in the column with the can because that is the column for words with the /ă/ sound."

5. Ask students to respond chorally to the next word, *mix*. Guide them as they tap out the word, and then place a star in the /ĭ/ column.

6. Orally, give students a series of words containing the target sounds.

↺ Ask students to repeat the words, tap the sounds, and then place a star in the correct column.

     ↺ Reinforce all words that may be new vocabulary by showing objects or using acting or gestures to reinforce oral language development.

7.   Have students take turns using the words in a sentence.

Independent Practice

For additional reinforcement, students can practice Star Sounds with a partner.

1.   Give each pair of students a bag of objects.

2.   Hand out the Star Sounds Worksheet with target sounds written at the top.

3.   Explain that partners will take turns removing an object from the bag and that each partner will put a star in the correct column of their worksheet to match the target sound of the object. (Objects can be presorted so they match the target sounds, or students can use their phonological skills to decide if the objects fit the target sounds. If the object does not fit, students can set aside the object and choose another.)

4.   Tell students to continue taking turns until all the objects are out of the bag.

Stretching Students' Learning

     ◎ Use more difficult phonics concepts, such as short vowels, digraphs, blends, vowel pairs, syllable types, or morphemes.

Listen and Clap

Activity Overview

Listen and Clap helps develop and reinforce students' ability to listen to and think about sounds in words. Additionally, it gives students opportunities to compare and make judgments about the sounds they hear. Listen and Clap connects students to the learning through multisensory engagement, which enhances the efficacy of the instruction.

Materials • • • • • •

- Plastic hand clappers* (*optional*)
- Alphabet guides
- Container with a selection of objects and small bags to hold the objects
- Whiteboard, dry-erase marker, and eraser
- Student whiteboards, dry-erase markers, and erasers
- Picture cards (simple pictures)

* Available in the optional Classroom Manipulatives Kit

Whole Classroom Instruction

Set the purpose. Say: "This activity gives you practice listening to the sounds in words. You will listen and then write the sound you hear at the beginning of the word for each object that is chosen. Being able to hear sounds in words and write the letters that stand for those sounds will help you to become good readers, writers, and spellers."

1. Sit in a circle on the floor with students (or they may be seated at their desks).

2. Distribute plastic clappers, if available, and alphabet guides to each student. Students can clap their hands for this activity (or do thumbs up, thumbs down) if you do not have clappers.

3. Choose an object from the container. Say the name of the object and ask students to repeat the name of the object.

4. Model the activity first. State the initial sound of the object (dog, /d/).

5. Ask students if they agree that the object starts with a /d/ sound. If they agree, tell them that they may clap their clappers. If they do not agree, they are to stay quiet. Give feedback to students about the accuracy of their response.

6. Next, write the first sound on a whiteboard. Say the sound as you write the *d;* mention that they can look at an alphabet guide and remember how to form the letter if they need to.

7. When you have completed the *d,* ask students to follow and write a *d* on their whiteboards.

8. Repeat the activity, having a student choose an object this time. Ask that student to state the name of the object and tell the class what the first sound is. The class once again decides if they agree or not and claps or is silent, depending on their judgment of the sound.

9. Ask the class to erase the *d* and then write the first sound they hear in the name of the new object. Remind them to check their alphabet guide if they need to.

Students agree by clapping their small plastic hand clappers.

10. Repeat this activity using the final sound or the middle sound if students are ready for that skill.

Return to the purpose. Say: "You've been practicing listening to, naming, and writing sounds in words. Being able to hear different sounds in words and write the letters that stand for those sounds will help you to be good readers, writers, and spellers."

Small Group Work

1. Distribute hand clappers, if available, and place picture cards face down in front of the group.

2. Ask a student to choose a picture card.

3. Have the student name the picture and then state the first sound in the name of the picture.

4. Instruct the other students in the group to follow the original procedure of agreeing or not agreeing with the sound given, using their clappers (or clapping their hands).

5. Tell everyone to write the sound on their whiteboards.

6. Have students take turns using the target word (the name of the picture) in a sentence.

7. Ask students to repeat Listen and Clap several times so that each student gets a few turns.

Independent Practice

Listen and Clap can be repeated with students working in pairs.

Talking Classroom

1. Give each pair of students a bag with objects in it.

2. Tell students to take turns removing something from the bag, naming the object, and then writing the letter that represents the beginning sound on their whiteboards.

3. Have students take turns using the word in a sentence.

Rhyming Rhythms

Activity Overview

The ability to rhyme is often thought of as related to future reading success. Rhyming may be considered predictive because the skills necessary for rhyming involve the ability to segment, blend, and manipulate sounds within words. This ability involves the core phonemic awareness skills that are related to success in reading and spelling. For instance, to change the word *fat* to *cat*, a student must be able to hear the initial sound, segment off the initial sound, and manipulate that sound by replacing the /f/ with a /k/ and then blend the sounds back together to create the new word, *cat*. Rhyming Rhythms is an activity that emphasizes the first necessary skill for rhyming: initial sound awareness.

Materials • • • • • •

- Instant whiteboards (made from card stock and plastic sheet protectors; see Rhyming Rhythms Worksheet in Appendix A), dry-erase markers, and erasers
- Objects (or pictures) that represent rhyming words (bat, cat; pig, wig)
- A large container and small bags to hold the objects
- Chart paper and marker

Whole Classroom Instruction

Set the purpose. Say: "Saying and reading rhyming words is fun and will help you listen for sounds in words. When you can hear and write the sounds in words and the letters that make those sounds, you will be able to read and write more easily."

Make instant whiteboards in advance using the Rhyming Rhythms Worksheet and sheet protectors.

1. Sit in a circle on the floor with students.

2. Distribute the instant whiteboards, markers, and erasers to everyone.

3. Choose an object from the container (a pig, for instance) and say the name of the object.

4. Ask students to say the name of the object. Discuss the vocabulary, building background knowledge as needed.

5. Begin to sing using the rhythm of "Old McDonald Had a Farm." You may use any other rhythm that your students would know or a lively rap rhythm. Insert the name of one of the students in the song and combine it with the sounds of the object that was selected:
    One day Lucy had a pig, /p/, /p/, /p/, /p/, /p/.
    One day Lucy had a pig, /p/, /p/, /p/, /p/, /p/.
    That pig was made of /p/ and /ig/, pig, pig, pig, pig, pig.
    That pig was made of /p/ and /ig/, pig, pig, pig, pig, pig.

6. State the initial sound of the object (/p/).

7. Model writing the initial sound of the word *pig* (/p/) on an instant whiteboard, and then ask students to write the initial sound on their instant whiteboards in the first box.

8. Model writing the rest of the word (/ig/) in the second box, segmenting and blending the word, and then ask students to write the rest of the word on their own boards.

9. Model using the word in a sentence: "The **pig** was pink and round." Show the class a wig and repeat the activity with the rhyming word *wig*.

10. Ask what part of the words *pig* and *wig* is the same. (The "ig" part.)

11. Repeat the activity, this time choosing another student and using the word *wig*, not *pig*:
    One day Jose had a wig, /w/, /w/, /w/, /w/, /w/.
    One day Jose had a wig, /w/, /w/, /w/, /w/, /w/.
    His wig was made of /w/ and /ig/, wig, wig, wig, wig, wig.
    His wig was made of /w/ and /ig/, wig, wig, wig, wig, wig.

12. Say: "Let's write the first sound of the word wig on your board in the first box." Students can then check their work against yours.

13. Next, say: "Let's read the ending part of the word *wig*." /ig/

14. Say: "Now, let's read the word together." With the class, segment and blend the word to read it.

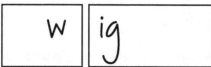

15. Say a sentence using the word *wig*: "I would like to wear a funny **wig**."

16. Ask students to turn to a neighbor and use the word *wig* in a sentence.

17. Tell students to compare the words *pig* and *wig* and see if they can find the part that is the same and the part that is different.

18. Have everyone erase the letters inside their boxes.

19. Do one more set of rhyming words following the same procedure.

Return to the purpose. Say: "You have been practicing listening for and writing the sounds in words. Being able to hear sounds and write the letters that make those sounds will make you good readers and writers."

Small Group Work

1. Distribute the instant whiteboards using the Rhyming Rhythms Worksheet, markers, and erasers to the group.

2. Say a word, such as *man*.

3. Ask students to think of a word that rhymes with *man*. Students may come up with *fan, tan, plan,* and *can*.

4. Write the students' words on chart paper.

5. Ask the group to choose two of the words they generated and copy them onto their whiteboards, separating the initial sound and the rhyming part of the word.

6. Have students compare their words and explain what part of the word is the same and what part is different.

7. Tell students to choose one of the words, turn to a neighbor, and use the word in a sentence. Repeat this step if time allows.

Independent Practice

Rhyming Rhythms can be repeated with students working in pairs.

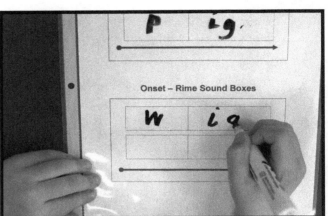

Onset – Rime Sound Boxes

1. Give students a bag with objects in it, instant whiteboards, markers, and erasers.

2. Tell them they can repeat the song you used during whole class instruction if they choose.

3. Have students take turns removing something from the bag, naming the object, and then writing the initial sound and a rhyme for each word on their instant whiteboards.

Stretching Students' Learning

◎ Have students read simple sentences that contain the patterns they have practiced in the Rhyming Rhythms activity.

Walkabout Sound Matching

Activity Overview

Walkabout Sound Matching helps develop and reinforce students' skill in identifying and matching initial sounds in words. This activity gives students opportunities to compare and contrast sounds and make judgments about those sounds. Lively opportunities to listen and think about sounds keeps students attentive and thereby deepens learning. Walkabout Sound Matching also focuses on the sound/symbol connection, which is critical for developing automaticity with the alphabetic code.

Materials • • • • • • •

- ◉ Picture cards or objects
- ◉ Letter cards (see Appendix B)
- ◉ Student whiteboards, dry-erase markers, and erasers

Whole Classroom Instruction

Set the purpose. Say: "You are going to practice listening for and matching the sounds in the names of different pictures and objects. Being able to hear sounds and discover sounds that match will help you to become good readers."

1. Distribute one picture card or object to each student. These will be used for matching initial sounds.

2. Hold up a picture or an object (such as a pot) and say the name of the object, "pot," and the initial sound in the word, "/p/."

3. Hold up other pictures or objects and have students name the initial sound in each.

4. Ask students, one at a time, to stand up with their picture and say the initial sound of the object shown. Have students remain standing.

5. Next, have one student walk around the room, holding his picture in front of him so that everyone can see it and can think about the beginning sound. When the student circling the room finds someone whose picture has an initial sound that matches his, he stands alongside that student. (The student who has the pie may stand next to the student who has the pin.)

6. Repeat this process two times, then ask students to walk around the room and find a picture that has a beginning sound that matches their own.

7. If time permits, collect the pictures, redistribute them, and repeat the activity.

Return to the purpose. Say: "Listening for sounds and discovering matching sounds will help you become good readers."

Small Group Work

For this part of the activity, you will be playing a game in which the students will be matching a letter card with a picture.

1. Place the decks of letter cards and pictures face down in front of the group.

2. Have the first student turn over one card from each deck. If the letter card doesn't match the initial sound of the picture, the student leaves both cards face up in the middle of the table and the next player takes two cards. If the student can make a match with any of the cards on the table, she takes the pair and leaves any card she doesn't use face up on the table for the next student to try to use.

3. Play continues with the next student.

4. The game ends when the cards have all been used. The student with the most pairs wins.

5. Choose two to three picture cards and model making sentences that include the objects. For example: "My **mother** cooked the **soup** in a big **pot**."

6. Tell students to take turns making sentences using two or three picture cards.

7. Challenge the students to work as a group and use as many picture cards as they can to incorporate into sentences.

Independent Practice

Repeat Walkabout Sound Matching with students working in pairs.

1. Distribute a deck of picture cards to each pair of students.

2. Ask students to take turns turning over a picture card.

3. Have them each use their whiteboard and marker to write the grapheme (letter or letters) that represents the initial sound of the object chosen. When finished, they are to place the card to the side, erase the grapheme, and repeat the procedure with another card.

4. After students have selected three or four cards, have them combine the cards and take turns orally creating sentences that use the words or concepts depicted in the pictures. For example, if a student uses the pictures of a girl jumping, a small dog, and a ball, he may create a sentence such as: The **dog** can **jump** over the **ball**.

Stretching Students' Learning

◎   Use more difficult phonics concepts, such as short vowels, digraphs, or ending sounds.

Concept Maps

Activity Overview

Concept maps are commonly used for comprehension instruction. However, they can also be very valuable for demonstrating the relationship between words that share common sounds. The Concept Maps activity uses graphic organizers designed to help students form concepts, in this case, about the sounds in words. The activity gives students an opportunity to compare and contrast sounds and explore words in relationship to other words they know. This activity should be part of an overall effort to enhance word consciousness by giving students points when they listen for a word in speech, watch for a word in print, and use the word in their speaking and writing.

Materials

- Card stock
- Letter cards (see Appendix B)
- Pictures that demonstrate target sounds
- Word Web Worksheet (see Appendix A)
- Student whiteboards, dry-erase markers, and erasers
- Chart paper and marker
- Index cards (or sticky notes) and colored pencils (or markers)

Whole Class Instruction

Set the purpose. Say: "You are going to practice listening to the names of various pictures. You will listen and then write the sounds you hear in each name. Being able to hear sounds and write the letters that stand for those sounds will help you to become better readers, writers, and spellers."

1. Introduce the target sound that is being taught, for example, beginning, ending, or middle sounds.

2. Create a "concept map" on the floor using card stock. See the next page for an example.

3. Place a letter card for the target sound in the center of the concept map, for example, *p*.

4. Place a picture that begins with the /p/ sound, like a pen, pencil, pig, purse, or pickle, in each section of the concept map.

5. Distribute one picture card to each student.

6. Ask students, one at a time, to decide if their picture fits in the concept map. If their card matches the target sound, the students take their card and stand in the part of the concept map that represents their sound.

   - Students may think of extra words to add. They can draw pictures to add to the map, like a pet or a peanut.

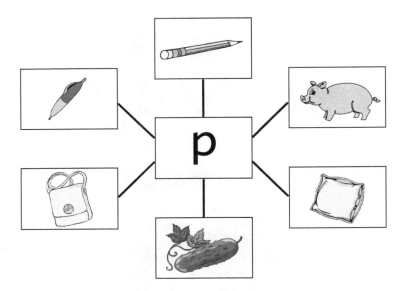

    ⚭ Students at their seats can copy the concept map onto a Word Web Worksheet or whiteboard while you copy it onto chart paper. Students may choose three pictures to put on their map.

7. Hang the concept map up on the wall as part of a phonemic awareness living word wall.

Return to the purpose. Say: "You have been practicing listening to the names of various pictures. You will listen and then write the sounds you hear in each name. Being able to hear sounds and write the letters that stand for those sounds will help you to become better readers, writers, and spellers."

Small Group Work

The Concept Maps activity can be continued in a small group by giving students more opportunities to listen for, watch for, and use the target sound and words.

This student is drawing pictures to complete a sound concept map. The pictures all start with the sound /b/.

1. Work alongside students to create a concept map, using the digraph /ch/, for example, as the target sound.

2. Give pairs of students in the group a Word Web Worksheet and colored pencils. Ask them to create a concept map by saying the words orally (such as *cheese*, *chop*, and *chocolate*) and then drawing pictures of those words.

Talking Classroom

3. Have students share their pictures and talk about their words and the sound that belongs in the concept map.

Independent Practice

This activity can be repeated with students working in pairs.

1. Give each pair of students a partially completed concept map on the Word Web Worksheet.

2. Ask students to complete the concept map on their own.

Stretching Students' Learning

- The difficulty level of the concept map can be increased to include short vowels, digraphs, blends, and other phonics concepts.

- Students can copy their concept maps.

- Students can write simple sentences using the sound words in their concept maps.

Faces of Our Friends

Activity Overview

Faces of Our Friends uses pictures of students in the class to stimulate and develop linguistic thinking. The activity gives students practice in phonemic processing at their individual levels. For example, students may be asked to segment the sounds in a friend's name or just give the first sound in the name. Phonemic segmentation and blending are critical subskills for proficient reading and spelling. This activity starts from a place of meaningful language comprehension (because students know one another) and builds phonological skills with meaningful and fun practice.

Materials • • • • • • •

- Small pictures of each child in the class mounted on tongue depressor sticks
- A container to hold the pictures face down
- Alphabet strip
- Student whiteboards, dry-erase markers, and erasers
- Small pictures of each child in class mounted on index cards (you might want to make multiple sets)
- Letter cards (see Appendix B)

Whole Classroom Instruction

Set the Purpose. Say: "Today you are going to practice listening for sounds in the names of your classroom friends. You will listen and then write some of the sounds you hear in each name. Being able to hear sounds and write the letters that stand for those sounds will help you to become good readers, writers, and spellers."

1. Have students sit in a circle on the floor.

2. Place the cards with students' pictures face down in a container.

3. Select a card with a student's face on it and say the student's name.

4. Tell the class to repeat the student's name.

5. Model tapping out the student's name using finger tapping. If, for instance, the student's name is *Matt*, tap out the sounds in *Matt*, /m/ /ă/ /t/.

6. Ask questions about the name, such as:
   - What is the first sound in *Matt*? (/m/)
   - What is the last sound in *Matt*? (/t/)
   - How many sounds do you hear in *Matt*? (three)

7. Say, "Matt begins with the letter *m*." Write the letter *m* on your whiteboard to model for the class.

8. Next, ask students to write the letter *m*.

9. Call on one or two students to say something nice about Matt.

10. Select another stick and proceed with the activity. Students can also choose the sticks.

Return to the purpose. Say:
"You've been practicing listening, naming, and writing the sounds in the names of your classroom friends. Being able to listen for, name, and write the sounds will help you to become good readers, writers, and spellers."

Small Group Work

In this portion of the activity, use the students' pictures to stimulate authentic conversations and sentence elaboration.

1. Arrange face down the cards with the pictures of the students in the group, and select one card.

2. Ask the group to tap out the sounds of the student's name whose face was chosen.

3. Next, have students write the initial sound of the student's name on their whiteboards.

4. Have the student whose face was chosen tell the group something that he or she likes to do.

5. Ask everyone in the group to say something about the student who is at the heart of the activity.

6. Have the student who is at the heart of the activity pick the next face, and repeat the activity.

Independent Practice

Repeat this activity with students working in pairs. This game could involve initial sounds, ending sounds, or middle sounds, depending on the students' skill level.

1. Give each pair of students a set of index cards that has classmates' faces glued on one side and another set of cards that have graphemes on them.

2. Have partners take turns turning over two cards—one from the face pile and the other from the grapheme pile. The cards are left face up on the table.

3. Explain that when a student turns over a card from one pile (such as /j/) that matches a card on the table from the other pile (e.g., *Jill*), the student gets to take the pair.

4. When a pair is taken, the partner who made the match must say a sentence about the person who they just matched.

5. The partner who has the most pairs wins the game.

Stretching Students' Learning

◉ Students could draw a picture of one of their classroom friends and list three things they like about that person.

Clothespin Sounds

dog

a b c d e f g h i j k l m
n o p q r s t u v w x y z

Activity Overview

Clothespin Sounds gives students practice listening to, matching, and identifying the sounds and the graphemes that represent those sounds. This activity strengthens phonological processing while reinforcing sound/symbol and orthographic knowledge. It also develops and reinforces vocabulary and oral language skills for English language learners or first language learners who have low language skills.

Materials • • • • • • •

- Alphabet strips with pictures
- Clothespins
- Student whiteboards, dry-erase markers, and erasers
- Container of objects

Whole Classroom Instruction

Set the purpose. Say: "This activity will give you practice matching sounds and letters. The more quickly and accurately you can match sounds and letters, the easier it will be for you to sound out words and spell words when you are writing."

1. Be sure students are seated in a manner in which they can clearly see what you are doing and feel engaged, such as a circle. Hold an alphabet strip so that students can see you model.

2. Give each student:
   - An alphabet strip that has pictures to accompany the letter sounds (or a more limited strip with selected graphemes on it, such as short vowels, digraphs, etc., depending on the skill level of the students).

a	b	c	d	e	f	g	h	i	j	k	l	m	n	o	p	q	r	s	t	u	v	w	x	y	z	
		sh				ch				th																
		s				k				t																

   - Three clothespins.

3. Hold up an object and say the name of the object, for instance, "pot."

4. Have students repeat the word, and make sure they understand the meaning of the word.

5. Model by saying, "I hear a /p/ sound at the beginning of the word *pot*."
   - Take a clothespin and place it over the *p* on your alphabet strip to model the action for students.

6. Have students take one of their clothespins and place it over the *p* or the picture on their alphabet strips.

7. Model writing a *p* on your whiteboard. Say the sound /p/ in a loud voice.

8. Write a *p* again and ask the class to also write the letter *p* on their whiteboards. End by saying the sound /p/ together in a loud voice.

9. Model by saying another word that begins with /p/. "Penny." Then, use "penny" in a sentence. "I found a **penny** on the street yesterday."

10. Have students turn to their neighbors and say one more word that starts with the sound /p/. Then ask students to make up a sentence with the new word they have thought of and share their sentence with their neighbor.

11. Repeat this activity three times with other objects or pictures and different sounds or with words presented orally.

Return to the purpose. Say: "You have been working on connecting letter sounds and letters. Being able to put sounds and letters together quickly will help you to be better readers, writers, and spellers."

Small Group Work

1. Distribute alphabet strips to students.

2. Point to a letter on your alphabet strip and ask students to say the correct sound.

3. Say another sound and ask students to point to the grapheme on their own alphabet strip that represents that sound.

4. Continue working on the same concept of rapid connection and recognition of sounds and letters.

5. Continue to work at the sound level. Point to various pictures or graphemes on your alphabet strip, and then ask students to give you the sound. For example, point to the grapheme *t* or the picture of the tent, and prompt students to say "/t/" as quickly as they can.

6. Choose a few words (such as *name* and *pen*) that can be incorporated into oral language practice. Have students use the words in sentences that relate to themselves. For example: "I feel grown-up when I write my **name** with a **pen**."

Independent Practice

Repeat Clothespin Sounds with students working in pairs this time. Students will take turns being the "teacher" and the "student."

1. Give both partners an alphabet strip, a container of objects to choose from, a clothespin, and a whiteboard and marker.

2. Have each partner choose five objects.

3. Tell the "teacher" to give the "student" one object, saying the name of the object.

4. Ask the "student" to repeat the name of the object and then proceed to put on her alphabet strip a clothespin on the first sound for that object.

5. Have both the "teacher" and the "student" write the grapheme on their whiteboards, saying the sound as they form the letter.

6. Let children switch roles of being the "teacher" and the "student," repeating the activity several times.

Stretching Students' Learning

- Use more difficult phonics concepts, such as short vowels, digraphs, blends, vowel pairs, syllable types, or morphemes (e.g., a picture of a shoe or a ship for the digraph /sh/, or a pot or a top for short-o sounds).

Flyswatter Sounds

Activity Overview

Flyswatter Sounds gives students practice listening to, identifying, and matching the sounds with the graphemes that represent those sounds. This activity strengthens the phonological processor while reinforcing sound/symbol and orthographic knowledge, building to mastery and automaticity in those areas. Flyswatter Sounds uses pictures that build vocabulary for the English language learner or first language learner who has low language skills. It emphasizes the development of speed and accuracy of initial sound and sound/symbol knowledge.

Materials • • • • • •

- Transparencies of simple pictures
- Overhead projector (or chart paper and masking tape)
- Flyswatters
- Picture cards
- Whiteboard or paper for score keeping

Whole Classroom Instruction

Set the purpose. Say: "In this activity, you will be practicing what you know about sounds in words. The more quickly and accurately you can recognize sounds and then match them with their letters, the easier it will be for you to sound out and spell words when you are writing."

1. Divide the class into two teams and have the teams line up on both sides of the room.

2. Display several simple pictures on the overhead projector (or mount on chart paper or the board using masking tape).

3. Call on one student from each team to approach the front of the room and give them both a flyswatter.

4. Say, for example, "Find the picture that starts with the same sound as *cup*."
   - The first student to swat the picture of a can with the flyswatter scores one point for his team.
   - If he can then label the picture correctly, he will get an extra point for his team.

5. Have the two students pass their flyswatters to the next students in line and then walk to the end of the line.

6. Repeat this activity until one team is the winner. Play for as long as time permits, giving each student two to three turns. The pacing should be fast and fun. The goal is to get to automatic recognition.

7. When students are ready, repeat Flyswatter Sounds with ending sounds and middle sounds, if appropriate.

Return to the purpose. Say: "You've been practicing matching sounds with pictures. The quicker you can recognize sounds in words, the easier it will be for you to read and spell."

Small Group Work

1. Place a deck of picture cards face down in front of the students. Sort the pictures to be sure they match the sounds you have been working on as a class.

2. Divide the group into two teams, and give one flyswatter to each team.

3. Determine what the students will be looking for. For example: "We are looking for a picture that starts with the same sound as *leg*."

4. Have someone from each team turn over a card at the same time until a picture comes up that starts with an /l/ sound: lamp.
   - The first person to swat the picture card that starts with /l/ gets a point.
   - For another point, the student must label the picture correctly. If the student does not know how to label the picture and his opponent can, the opponent would earn a point for her team.
   - Two new team members then begin turning cards to match a new sound.
   - Play continues so that there is rapid practice with multiple opportunities for sound matching.

5. Choose three of the picture cards (for instance, lamp, peach, and rope) and place them on the table in front of students. Ask students to use the words in sentences, working together with their team. Examples: "We have a tall **lamp** at our house." "The **peach** is not ripe." "The **rope** belongs to my brother."

6. Have students share their sentences with the group. If they have used the word correctly, their team gets a point. The team with the most points wins.

Independent Practice

Have students work in pairs for more practice with Flyswatter Sounds. If the students cannot read, they should still be able to play independently because they can recognize the pictures and pay attention to the sounds. Pairing students who have limited vocabulary with students who could help them develop vocabulary is a helpful strategy.

1. Give each pair of students a deck of picture cards and a flyswatter.

2. Tell students whether they will be matching a beginning, ending, or middle sound as they play. For example, "You will be looking for pictures that have the same ending sounds as *book, pan, pickle, fish, bike,* and *slinky.*"

3. Have students continue to turn over the cards until they come upon a word that has a matching ending sound. For example: a picture of a bike matches the ending sound in *book*. The student who makes a correct match and swats the card the fastest earns a point.

4. The game ends when students have matched all the sounds you have asked them to match. Have students keep score on a whiteboard or a piece of paper.

Stretching Students' Learning

◉ The level of play can be increased to include short vowels, digraphs, blends, and other phonics concepts.

Phonics Activities

11. Tap It, Map It, and Graph It

12. Physical Phonics

13. I'm Magic *e*

14. Language Links

15. Picture Perfect Spelling

16. Syllable Tracking

17. Clothespin Phonics

18. Where Is the Sound?

19. Flip Over Sounds

20. Walkabout Words

Phonics is the study of the system in which the sounds of our language are mapped into print. Teaching phonics strategies provides an important building block in the foundation of reading for students. The goal of phonics instruction is to give students insight into the sound/symbol relationship of our language.

Advanced phonics skills involve looking for and recognizing chunks in words, decoding them, and finally blending them back together to make meaningful multisyllabic words. To help students become proficient readers of multisyllabic words, instruction should include giving students insight into the morphemes (meaningful parts of words), the sound/symbol connections of phonemes (speech sounds), graphemes (letters and letter combinations that represent those sounds), and syllables in the English language. Teaching students to look for and understand those orthographic units in big words can be a very effective way to develop and improve the ability to read big words.

The activities in this section provide practice at both the simple phonics level (with basic sound/symbol and one-syllable word practice) and the syllable and morpheme level to advance students' ability to read multisyllabic words.

The Four Processing Systems Connection

The phonics activities are designed to involve the orthographic and phonological processors as students see a word and connect sounds to the symbols. The more students know about a word, the more automatically they can read that word. Therefore, the activities are designed to also engage the meaning and context processors to increase the students' ability to read the words fluently.

The LETRS Connection

◎ *Language Essentials for Teachers of Reading and Spelling* (LETRS), Module 3—*Spellography for Teachers: How English Spelling Works.*

◎ LETRS, Module 7—*Teaching Phonics, Word Study, and the Alphabetic Principle.*

◎ LETRS, Module 10—*Reading Big Words: Syllabication and Advanced Decoding.*

Phonics Activities

37

The Assessment Connection

- ꩜ *DIBELS: Dynamic Indicators of Basic Early Literacy Skills.* Oral Reading Fluency: Measures whether students can read connected text accurately and fluently.

- ꩜ *DIBELS: Dynamic Indicators of Basic Early Literacy Skills.* Nonsense Word Fluency: Measures whether students can name letter sounds and blend sounds to read unfamiliar words with short vowels in consonant-vowel-consonant or vowel-consonant syllable patterns.

- ꩜ *The CORE Phonics Survey.*

- ꩜ *The LETRS Phonics Surveys,* Modules 7 and 12.

- ꩜ TOWRE. The *Test of Word Reading Efficiency* (TOWRE) is a nationally normed measure of word reading accuracy and fluency.

The ELL Connection

Many of the activities in this section will be effective with ELLs without any alteration. However, a few small changes can have a great impact on the achievement and skill development for these students. The following are a few ideas to try that may enhance the effectiveness of the phonics activities:

- ꩜ Reading and spelling that is done at the sound level can be done effectively at the syllable level as well (for example, in the activity Tap It, Map It, and Zap It).

- ꩜ Adapt simple word work activities to the needs of ELLs by pairing a picture with a word students are building with letter tiles.

- ꩜ Extend word work learning by having students echo (repeat) each word before using it for phonics skill building.

- ꩜ Teaching morphology directly and systematically helps students decode meanings of big words.

- ꩜ When teaching morphology, it is helpful to directly teach the common morphological units between languages (e.g., shared roots). Teaching directly (rather than assuming the student will catch similarities) will increase students' awareness of shared linguistic features.

- ꩜ Activities that are done with an alphabet strip can also be done with a syllable strip, using whatever syllables are being directly taught.

- ꩜ Group and partner work provides modeling for oral language that is helpful to ELLs. In addition, the small group and partner settings offer environments that encourage more risk taking in the area of oral language.

- ꩜ Older students who are transitioning to English sometimes lack adequate direct, systematic instruction in the alphabetic code of English because such instruction is often emphasized in earlier grades. Speed drills can give students opportunities for extra practice after direct instruction has been given in the concepts of the code.

Dig In to Learn More

Henry, M. (2003). *Unlocking literacy: Effective decoding and spelling instruction*. Baltimore: Paul Brookes Publishing.

Moats, L. C. (2000). *Speech to print: Language essentials for teachers*. Baltimore, MD: Paul H. Brookes Publishing.

Tap It, Map It, and Graph It

Activity Overview

Phoneme-grapheme mapping is a multisensory and engaging technique for teaching sound-letter correspondences. In Tap It, Map It, and Graph It, students have opportunities to link the oral level phoneme as it is mapped to print in the form of a grapheme. Practice using this critical phonics skill can lead to greater mastery and automaticity in reading and spelling. Direct, explicit, and systematic instruction in the sound/symbol connection within the English alphabetic code helps students understand the relationship between phonemes and graphemes that exist in our complex spelling system. This activity draws the connection using tangible markers and letters and brings to life what could be a more abstract concept for students.

Materials •••••••

- ◎ Sound Box Worksheet (see Appendix A) placed in a plastic protective sleeve
- ◎ Dry-erase markers
- ◎ Objects that can be used as sound markers (cereal, counters, pennies, cut-up colored paper squares, etc.)
- ◎ Copies of decodable text
- ◎ Magnetic wands and magnetic discs*

* Available in the optional Classroom Manipulatives Kit

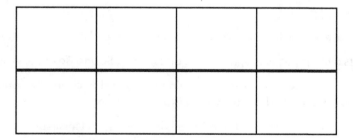

Whole Classroom Instruction

Set the purpose. Say: "This activity will give you practice matching sounds in words to the letters that go with those sounds. Thinking about sounds and the letters that represent those sounds is important to being a good reader and speller."

1. Give students copies of the Sound Box Worksheet and sound markers.

2. Begin at the phonemic awareness level: Say a given word and have the students repeat the word.

   - ◔ **Tap It**: Students may tap out the word first if needed, and then place a sound marker in each square of the grid for each sound they hear. (Each marker represents a sound in the word you say.) For example, if the word is *sheep*, the students repeat the word then tap out the sounds in the word.

  ℮ **Map It**: Have students move one marker into each box of the grid, with each marker representing a sound in the word: /sh/ /ē/ /p/ = three markers.

3. Next, add the graphemes that represent the sounds.

  ℮ **Graph It**: Students tap the word then write the graphemes in the appropriate boxes below the sound markers.

  ℮ Ultimately the goal is for students to be able to map the graphemes without needing to use the sound markers first. Some students will benefit from continuing to use the sound markers in association with the graphemes to make a clear visual representation of sound-symbol relationships.

  ℮ To vary the activity, have students remove the markers one sound at a time and write the corresponding graphemes for each marker, thereby replacing the marker with a written grapheme.

Return to the purpose. Say: "You have been practicing matching sounds and letters. Getting faster at that will help you to be better readers and spellers."

Small Group Work

Whenever possible, use words from books that students are reading.

1. Give students a magnetic wand, magnetic discs, and a Sound Box Worksheet.

2. Tell students to listen to a word you are going to say and to count the sounds by placing discs in the boxes provided on the Sound Box Worksheet.

3. Have students use the wand (or their fingers, if wands aren't available) to lift each disc, one at a time, and write in its place a grapheme that matches that sound.

  ℮ A variation of this activity is to have students leave the discs in place and, in the row beneath them, write the graphemes that match the sounds.

Independent Practice

For this portion of the activity, students will work in pairs, taking turns being the "teacher" and the "student."

1. Distribute copies of text, the Sound Box Worksheet, markers, magnetic wands, and discs.

2. Tell students to go into the text and select a word for their partner to tap, map, and graph.

3. Explain that each partner will take turns being the "teacher" and the "student" as they complete this activity, using the materials in the same manner as they did in their small group work.

4. Ask students to take the words they have been working with and use three of them in sentences. Ask each student to choose one of their sentences to write, using a dry-erase marker, on the bottom of their worksheet. Then, have students read their sentences to their partners.

Stretching Students' Learning

◎ Use increasingly complex words for sound mapping.

◎ Students can replace sound markers with letters, zapping the markers one at a time and writing the appropriate letter in its place, or leaving the markers down on the first row of boxes and writing the appropriate grapheme under the sound marker that it matches.

◎ Use multisyllabic words with the markers representing syllables.

Physical Phonics

Activity Overview

Students learn best when they are engaged in the learning process. It is our job as teachers to present material in ways that encourage the full attention and participation of our students. Physical Phonics is a multisensory activity that reinforces phonics concepts that have been previously introduced in the reading curriculum. This activity gives students fun opportunities to think about and analyze phonics concepts as they build words, write words, and compare their linguistic thinking to the thinking of others in the class.

Materials • • • • • • •

- ◎ Plastic hand clappers* (or noisemakers) (*optional*)
- ◎ Cards printed with letters and/or syllables
- ◎ Student whiteboards, dry erase markers, and erasers
- ◎ Cards that have prefixes, roots or base words, and suffixes (*optional*)
- ◎ Folders (laminated, if possible)
- ◎ Sticky notes
- ◎ Dry-erase markers
- ◎ Picture cards (*optional*)

* Available in the optional Classroom Manipulatives Kit

Whole Classroom Instruction

Set the purpose. Say: "In this activity, you will practice what you have learned about sounds and letters by building and writing words. Knowing about sounds and letters will make you better readers and spellers."

1. Give a hand clapper to each student, if available.

2. Distribute cards with a predetermined set of letters or syllables on them (one set on each card). For example: "m, t, p, a, o, s."

3. Have students with cards come to the front of the class.

4. Tell students at their desks to write a given word, such as *map* (formed using the same letters that students at the front of the class have on their cards), on their whiteboards.

5. Ask students at the front of the room to build the word *map* with their cards. Holding their respective card, have them stand next to each other in an order that forms the word. Then have them say the word—first segmenting, then blending: /m/ /ă/ /p/; *map*.

6. Have students at their desks compare and contrast what they wrote with the students at the front of the class. If they agree, they clap their hand clappers (or clap their hands). If they disagree, they are silent.

7. Next, instruct students at their desks to create a new word on their whiteboard, *mop,* and repeat the rest of the process.

  ℮ This activity can be done at different levels of difficulty. For example, it could be done with vowel pairs, such as "ai," and changing *main* to *rain* to *train.*

  ℮ The activity can also be done with morphemes. Distribute cards that have prefixes, roots or base words, and suffixes, such

  as *re-, tell, mind, lax,* and *-ing.* Your instructions might be: "Change *retell* to *retelling,* and now to *reminding,* next to *relaxing,* and finally to *relax.*"

Return to the purpose. Say: "You have been practicing working with sounds and letters by building and writing words. That kind of practice will make you better readers and spellers."

Small Group Work

1. Ask students to draw a line down the middle of their whiteboards, forming two columns.

2. At the top of each column have students write a phonics concept that is being practiced, such as /ă/ and /ŏ/.

3. Say words one at a time and have students tap out the sounds in each word, tapping harder on the middle tap to emphasize the vowel, and then write the word in the column that matches the sound. For example, *nap* would be written in the column marked *a.*

  ℮ For advanced students: At a syllabic level, the column headings could be open syllables and closed syllables and the words could be *mob, go, she, trick,* etc.

4. Use a few of the words in a sentence and then have the students "code" the sentence for the target phonics concept. For example, have students draw a circle around the word with the /ŏ/ sound and a square around the words with the /ă/ sound.

5. Tell students to choose one or two words from the lists they have made and turn to a neighbor and use those words in sentences.

Independent Practice

Have students form pairs to practice this activity.

1. Distribute folders and sticky notes to each student. (Laminating the folders ahead of time is helpful.)

2. Using the same target concepts that you used for the small group work, ask students to write words on sticky notes that use these two target concepts (e.g., short vowels *a* and *o*). Students might write *cap/top/hot/snap/trap/chop.* You can ask students to look in their reading books to find words.

3. Have students:

Talking Classroom

- ↻ Make two columns, labeling each as they did during the small group work, and sort the sticky notes under the appropriate column.
- ↻ Create two sentences using the words, one from each list. Tell them to share their sentences orally with each other and then write them on the bottom half of the folder.
- ↻ Code the words using a similar method introduced in the small group work.

4. For advanced students, use prefixes, suffixes, and roots (e.g., *re*, *pre* with *mind*, *test*) or syllable types (e.g., closed syllables *ex*, *land*, with magic *e* syllables *plode*, *slide*).

Stretching Students' Learning

- ◉ Use increasingly complex words, syllable patterns, and morphemes for sound mapping.

I'm Magic e*

onsonant

Activity Overview

I'm Magic *e* actively engages students in making and reading words using letter cards. It stresses the core phonological skill of blending and segmenting sounds and offers practice in manipulating sounds. This word-building activity helps to strengthen letter/sound knowledge and orthographic patterns, thereby promoting automaticity with important reading skills. As students work on building words, I'm Magic *e* can also be used to emphasize vocabulary and contextual understanding of the words being built.

Materials......

- Letter cards mounted on green, yellow, and red construction paper plus a magic *e* card mounted on another color
- Three baskets (red, yellow, and green, if possible) to hold the letter cards
- Plastic hand clappers (*optional*)
- Magic *e* hat (e.g., a wizard's cap, or some other special hat)
- Student whiteboards, dry-erase markers, and erasers
- Letter cards (see Appendix B)
- Speed Drill Worksheet (see Appendix A)
- Pictures or objects (*optional*)

Whole Classroom Instruction

Set the purpose. Say: "Today you are going to build words using letter cards. You will be writing down the words and then using those words in sentences. As you practice word building, reading and writing will get easier."

Prior to the activity, sort the letter cards into three baskets:

- First basket: beginning consonants, digraphs, and initial blends mounted on green paper (representing the beginning of the word). Letters should be chosen depending on what has already been taught.

- Middle basket: vowels or vowel teams mounted on yellow paper (representing the middle sound).

- Third basket: ending consonants, digraphs, and ending blends mounted on red paper (representing the end of the word).

*Adapted with permission from the work of Kass Patterson, teacher at Colorado Academy.

1. Distribute plastic hand clappers, if available, to everyone.

2. Choose three students to stand behind the baskets of letter cards and a fourth student to sit in a chair wearing the magic *e* hat and holding a magic *e* card face down.

3. Have the first student pick a green initial consonant card, the second student pick a yellow middle vowel card, and the third student pick a red final consonant card.

4. One at a time, ask the three students who are standing to say their individual sounds and then blend their sounds together (using the short vowel sound).

5. Give extra support as needed by modeling segmenting and blending the sounds using finger tapping signals—for example, /t/ /ă/ /p/ = *tap*.

6. Have students at their desks tap out the word, blend it, and then write the word *tap* on their whiteboards (tapping again to help with spelling, if needed).

7. Tell the student holding the magic *e* card to stand, hold the magic *e* card up to face the class, and say loudly what is on her card, such as, "I'm Magic *e*, and "*a*" says /ā/!"

8. Have the students who are standing once again say their sounds, segmenting and blending, but this time ask the student with the vowel (yellow card) to use the long *a* sound to form the new word—*tape*.

   ☙ If the students at their seats agree with the student at the front of the room, they will clap their clappers (or clap their hands) in agreement.

   ☙ This act of thinking about the linguistic and orthographic elements of the word will deepen the connection to the concept and, therefore, the learning.

9. Next, ask the students to make the change on their whiteboards, changing their word from *tap* to *tape* and then saying the new word aloud.

10. Ask students if *tap* is a real word. Then ask if someone can make a sentence using the word *tape*.

11. Choose four new students to come up and stand in front with the baskets and magic *e* cards. Repeat the activity a few more times.

Return to the purpose. Say:
"You have been building words using letter cards. As you practice word building, reading and writing will get easier."

Small Group Work

You will use three small decks of letter cards and a deck of magic *e* cards for this portion of the activity. Each deck of letter cards has either a beginning, middle, or ending sound on the cards. The color coding used previously can be faded out for this repetition, working toward

more transference toward black-and-white print. However, if a student needs more support, the letters can either be written in green, yellow, and red markers or on the color-coded construction paper. One magic *e* card will be turned over when it is time to flex from the short vowel to the long vowel sound.

1. Place the three decks of letter cards and the deck of magic *e* cards in front of each student.

2. Have students take turns turning over three letter cards from their decks in front of them and arranging them into a word. Tell them to put a finger under each sound, pointing as they segment and then blend the word. Have students take turns until each has read the word they have constructed from the letter cards. The whole group should echo the word and repeat the word segmented, then blended.

3. Next, tell each student, one at a time, to turn over the magic *e* card. Instruct the first student to recode his word with the magic *e* card, making the first vowel a long sound, and say the new word aloud.

4. After each word is recoded and blended, ask if the word is real or make-believe. If it is real, choose one student to use the word in a sentence.

5. Repeat this activity several times.

6. Distribute a prepared speed drill grid to everyone in the group; take two to three minutes to have the students work on the speed drill as a group, with words that flex between short vowel and long vowel (magic *e*) words. Set a timer for 60 seconds. Point to the words, and have students read as many as they can before the timer goes off. Repeat for another minute to see if students can read more words the second time.

Independent Practice

For continued practice with I'm Magic *e*, have students work with a partner.

1. Distribute three piles of cards, a magic *e* card, and a blank sheet of paper to each pair of students. The three piles should consist of beginning consonants, short vowels, and ending consonants.

2. Have students make two columns on the top half of their paper and label the columns "short vowel" and "magic e."

3. Have students form words as they did during the small group activity, then record each short-vowel word in the short-vowel column (closed syllable) and to record each long vowel word (magic *e*) in the magic *e* column.

4. Have students choose three of the words and create sentences at the bottom of their pages.

Stretching Students' Learning

◉ Use two-syllable words that make use of the magic *e* pattern, such as *explode, devote, relate, decide,* and *sublime.*

Language Links

Activity Overview

The Language Links activities stress the connections between words. By creating networks of words, these activities help students learn words that are related to each other, leading to increased word learning. Connecting new learning to previously learned concepts helps retention and retrieval. Thinking about and practicing skills in related units helps expand the utility and flexibility of the knowledge and the instruction.

Materials . . . .

- Blank name badges
- Masking tape and marker
- Word cards
- Index cards
- Construction paper links for making paper chains
- Long sheet of paper
- Word Chain Worksheet (see Appendix A)

Whole Classroom Instruction

Set the purpose. Say: "Language Links is an activity that will help you to see the connections between words. When you learn words in relationship to other words, you can learn more words. Practicing this activity will make you better readers and writers."

Create a Living Chain With Word Badges

One variation of this activity involves literally building a living chain by having each student have a word in a name badge that hangs around his or her neck.

1. Distribute name badges to every student.

2. Tell students to mill about the room finding classmates to link to and creating a chain with other students whose words are "linked" physically to the other students in relation to the word structure, such as words containing the double vowel combination *ai*: (*rain, pail, sail, jail, brain,* etc.).

   - This can also be done linking words based on morphological word structure, such as words containing the prefix *re-* (*redo, rewrite, retell, react,* etc.) or the suffix *-ing* (*jumping, running, hopping, reading*).

Sample Phonics Concepts That Create a Living Chain

Short *i* Word	Chaining	Prefix *re-*	Short Vowel Words About Pets
pin	pin	reform	vet
pit	pan	replay	pet
bit	pat	recopy	dog
sit	pet	retell	cat
sip	pot	rewrite	pig

Living Links

Another whole class variation of Language Links can be done as follows:

1. Place two pieces of card stock on the wall, a few feet from each other. Label each one for the phonics concept you will be practicing, such as *ai* words and *ay* words.

2. Give six students a card that shows a word demonstrating one of the two phonics concepts you are practicing, such as *sail, tail, pay, play,* etc.

3. Give students who did not receive cards with words on them one blank index card.

4. As a group, create a bank of *ai* and *ay* words. To do this, have students brainstorm words that have the long *a* sound. Put those words on chart paper, under columns labeled *ai* and *ay*.

5. Call on the students who have the cards with words on them to come up and put themselves in a group by the phonics concept that corresponds to their card. Tell students to read their word to the class.

6. Ask students at their desks to choose an *ai* or *ay* word from the bank and write it on their index card.

7. Have students with index cards move one at a time to the group whose phonics concept matches the correct spelling they have written. For instance, all the students who have written *ai* words on their index card (*rain, pain, pail, hail, jail, sprain,* etc.) will go to the group with *ai* words. All the students who have written *ay* words on their cards (*pay, say, stay, stray, may*) will join the *ay* group.

Return to the purpose. Say: "You've been learning about words in relationship to other words. When you see connections between words, you will become good readers and writers."

Small Group Work

1. Distribute a Word Chain Worksheet to everyone in the group.

2. Place a long sheet of paper in the middle of the table and draw five links of a chain.

3. Take a stack of word cards that all contain the target concept, for instance, short *i* sounds, and place them on the drawn links of the chain (e.g., *wig, tin, lid, sit, big*).

Talking Classroom

4. Ask students to copy the words onto their Word Chain Worksheet.

5. With the students, generate several sentences that use some of the words in the links. Model good sentences and restate correctly sentences that are incorrect, giving positive and corrective feedback for students as they get opportunities for guided oral language practice. For example: "The girl has a **big wig**."

6. Write some of the sentences on the board and, with the children's input, code them for the target concept words. For instance, the coding may involve putting a circle around all the words with the short *i* sound. This allows for reinforcement of the activity before the children are asked to do it independently.

Independent Practice

This part of the activity involves both individual and partner work.

1. Give students a copy of the Word Chain Worksheet with one word written in the chain to get them started.

2. Explain which skill they will be practicing in their chain (phonics, vocabulary, or a morphological concept).

3. When the word chain is filled in with related words, have students choose three of the words to use in sentences and write them at the bottom of their worksheet. For instance, "I like to **sit with** my **little** pup."

4. Next, ask them to code the sentences for any short *i* word they have used.

5. Have students work with a partner and share the sentences they have created.

Stretching Students' Learning

- Use increasingly complex words, syllable patterns, and morphemes.

- Creating a word chain is also a useful strategy in vocabulary instruction and comprehension instruction, where students can link words that relate to a character, a problem, or to expository text information.

Students hold cards that are linked by the initial letter *c*, the sound /k/, and by concept (they are all animals).

Picture Perfect Spelling

Activity Overview

The more students know about a word, the better they will be able to read, understand, and spell the word. Good spellers use information about orthographic patterns, morphology, and phonemic awareness in order to write words correctly. Picture Perfect Spelling is an activity that takes the phonemic awareness skills that students have developed and applies them to spelling as a primary building block of word knowledge. It then focuses attention on known orthographic patterns and finally on unknown or unusual spelling patterns. This activity involves helping students "code" words in color that are being studied for spelling practice. It helps identify that which is known and that which is new and needs to be studied. Linking new information to previously learned information is a strategy that enhances new learning.

Materials • • • • • • •

- ◉ Whiteboard (or chart paper), dry-erase markers (green, red, and black), and eraser
- ◉ Student whiteboards, dry-erase markers (green, red, and black), and erasers
- ◉ Pictures (*optional*)
- ◉ Picture Perfect Spelling Worksheet (see Appendix A)
- ◉ Green and red colored pencils

Whole Classroom Instruction

Set the purpose. Say: "In this activity, you will be combining what you already know about sounds and letters with new things you will be learning about letter patterns. The more you know about words, the better you will be able to read, understand, and spell the words."

Use a spelling list based on a new orthographic pattern or morpheme pattern that you have taught. The list can also include a few irregular words that need to be learned.

1. On a whiteboard, write the spelling list, coding the first few words in green and red: green for the parts that are already known or can be figured out through sound tapping, and red for the new parts that are being learned or the parts that might not "play fair." For example:

    night
    fight
    bright
    flight

2. Say the first word. Tap it out. Ask the students to say the word and tap it after you.

    ↻ Talk about the part that plays fair and the part that is new to the students. Explain that the parts of the word that play fair are written in green and the parts that are new (or do not play fair) are written in red.

    ↻ Ask students to copy the word onto their whiteboards.

3. Have students read the next word and tap it out.

    ↻ Remind students that the parts written in green are the ones that can be discovered through sound tapping.

    ↻ Although the /ī/ sound in *fight* can be heard, its spelling is the part that is tricky. Therefore, it is written in red because red means "stop and think." It is the part that cannot be discovered through tapping but needs to be studied and remembered.

    ↻ Continue practicing in the same manner.

4. Discuss vocabulary as it is appropriate, supplementing the spelling words with pictures, gestures, or explanations as needed for students whose language is weak or for English language learners.

Return to the purpose. Say: "You have been combining what you already know about sounds and letters with new things you are learning about letter patterns. Practicing this activity can help you become better spellers."

Small Group Work

Use the same spelling word study list (but continue with words that were not coded in the whole group) or use a study list that contains other words with similar patterns.

1. Distribute the Picture Perfect Spelling Worksheet to everyone in the group.

2. Have students read the first word, tap it out, then code it in color (using red and green dry-erase markers) on their whiteboards.

3. Continue the activity with all the list words, repeating the procedure.

    ↻ This activity can be done with simple phonics-concept words or words that have prefixes, suffixes, and roots. For example:

        Prefix focus: <u>re</u>write, <u>re</u>tell, <u>re</u>mind, <u>re</u>do
        Suffix focus: jump<u>ing</u>, danc<u>ing</u>, sing<u>ing</u>, look<u>ing</u>
        Root focus: trans<u>form</u>, re<u>form</u>, in<u>form</u>, uni<u>form</u>

Talking Classroom

4. When all the words have been written, have students turn to their neighbor and choose a word to use in a sentence that expresses some connection they have with one of the words (such as *uniform*). For example: "I have a **uniform** I wear when I play soccer."

5. Using their Picture Perfect Spelling Worksheet, tell students to write the list of study words in the first column ("Word List").

6. In the middle column ("Write the Word in Color") ask them to write the first word using their colored pencils.

↺ Guide them to tap the word first and then decide which part they know (green) and on which part they will be focusing their study (red).

↺ Guide students to close their eyes and visualize the word in color.

7. Finally, have students fold their worksheet so that only the third column ("Rewrite the Word") is showing, and rewrite the original word in regular pencil, all one color.

8. Explain that students will be repeating this process to complete the list in their independent practice.

Independent Practice

Students will work independently and then with a partner to complete the activity.

1. Instruct the students to use their Picture Perfect Spelling Worksheet to continue working through the same procedure described in small group work, with all the words on their study list.

2. After they complete the list, have students work with a partner and orally test each other, reviewing the words together first—reading, tapping, closing the eyes to visualize, and then covering the word to try to recall the spelling.

3. Last, tell students to ask each other to give the correct spelling of each word.

Stretching Students' Learning

◉ Use multisyllabic words as well as words with more complex morphemic patterns, color coding syllables, and morpheme patterns as students study the words.

Syllable Tracking

Activity Overview

Teaching students to read big words is an important step in literacy instruction. Although the strategy of "sound it out" is effective for single-syllable words, the working memory of the typical reader's brain cannot hold the number of sounds in multisyllabic words. Therefore, "sound it out" doesn't work well for big words. To make multisyllabic words easier to read, we need to teach students to "chunk" the words and then decode and read those chunks to blend the word back together again.

Strategy instruction has proven to be a real asset to decoding instruction for all phonics learning. This involves teaching students about morphemes (meaningful parts of words), sound/symbol connections of phonemes (speech sounds), graphemes (letters and letter combinations that represent those sounds), and the code of syllables in the English language. Teaching students to look for and understand those units in big words can be very effective in improving reading.

Materials

- Index cards with word parts written on them
- Magnetic tape
- Whiteboard
- Word part cards (colored-coded with green, black, and red printing, *optional*)
- File folders
- Syllable Sorting Worksheet (see Appendix A)
- Sticky notes
- Chart paper and marker (*optional*)
- Resealable plastic bags
- Student whiteboards, dry-erase markers, and erasers

Often children with weaknesses at the early phonological stages have weaknesses again when it comes time to read multisyllabic words. Syllable Tracking is an activity that makes the parts of words concrete so that students get a deeper understanding of the way big words are built. Syllable tracking is listening to big words and finding the chunks, or word parts (syllables) that make up the word.

Whole Classroom Instruction

Set the purpose. Say: "This activity will help you to read big words by looking for word parts, or chunks, you have already learned about. When you can 'chunk' words based on the parts or syllable patterns that are familiar to you, it will be easier to read big words."

Prior to the activity, choose word parts that have been previously taught, and write them on 12 to 15 index cards. The parts will be syllables, prefixes, and roots or suffixes. Apply magnetic tape to the back of each card.

1. Using a whiteboard (or the floor), arrange the cards in three columns: prefixes in the left column, roots and other syllable types in the middle column, and ending syllables or suffixes in the right column.

2. Ask students to read and identify each syllable (receptive and expressive practice). For example, have them read the prefixes *trans-, sub-,* and *inter-* aloud with you. Then you will say the first prefix, *trans-,* and ask one student to come to the whiteboard and put his finger on *trans-*.

This student is building big words from word parts.

3. Create a word (it can be a nonsense word) using one prefix, root, and suffix, such as *trans-form-able*.

4. Read the word—segmenting and then blending—using the touch-and-say strategy. (Put a finger under each segment and say it. After all segments have been read, go back, run a finger under the whole word, and blend and read the word together.)

   ↻ Tell the class that you can change *transformable* to make a new word. Say, "I can change *transformable* to *interformable*." (If students are only ready to do two-syllable words, you may change *transform* to *translate*.)

   ↻ Take out the prefix *trans-* and replace it with the prefix *inter-* and read the new word by touching each syllable first then going back and blending the parts together to make the whole word.

   ↻ Ask the class what you would need to do to change *interformable* to *interportable*. The class will notice that you will need to take out the root *form* and replace it with the root *port.* Call on someone to come up and make the change.

5. Have the class read the word chorally—first segmenting and then blending.

6. Give several students word part cards that match what you have on the whiteboard. (The cards can be color coded: prefixes printed in green or mounted on green paper; middle syllables printed in black or mounted on black paper; and ending syllables written in red or mounted on red paper.)

7. Call students with cards up to the front of the room. Have those with prefixes line up behind the student who has *re-;* students with roots and middle syllables line up behind the student who has the root *port;* and students with the ending syllables line up behind the student who has the syllable *-ing.*

8. Repeat the syllable tracking process used with the previous activity.

   ↻ Ask the class which student has to move out in order to change the word *reporting* to *importing.*

   ↻ This process can be repeated with a chaining process: *importing—transporting—transport—report—reported,* etc. Explain that sometimes students may be forming nonsense words in which the spelling may not be correct, but for now the class is merely practicing reading big words by looking and holding the chunks in the words.

Return to the purpose. Say: "You have been reading big words by looking for the word parts, or chunks, you have already learned about. Chunking words makes it easier to read big words. You can chunk words based on meaningful parts of the words or syllable patterns."

Small Group Work

Syllable instruction can be reinforced with a syllable sorting activity in a small group.

1. Distribute file folders, the Syllable Sorting Worksheet, and sticky notes.

2. Instruct students to place their worksheet on one half of the inside of their folder.

3. On the front board (or chart paper), make a chart to reflect what the students will be working on. For example:

Closed Syllables	Open Syllables	Magic *e* Syllables
at	po	oke
pin	me	ate

4. Begin writing a list of syllables to match the syllable types you are working on. Generate one short list for each syllable type.

5. Ask the students to generate more syllables, about five for each type, and write them on the whiteboard.

6. Have students copy the syllables onto sticky notes (one to a note) and then take the sticky notes and place them in a mixed-up order on the other half of their folder.

7. Tell students to exchange folders with a neighbor, unscramble and sort the syllables by type, then place the sticky note in the proper column.

Independent Practice

Students will form pairs and will take turns being the "teacher" and the "student" in creating and changing words. This variation of Syllable Tracking can be differentiated based on the syllables learned of the six syllables types (closed, open, silent *e*, *r*-controlled, consonant + *le*, and vowel pair). If a student has learned only about open and closed syllables, then the tracking activity can be done with words composed of those syllable types, such as *ho-bo, mo-tel, mus-ic,* or *fan-tas-tic.*

1. Distribute resealable plastic bags with word parts to each pair of students.

2. Tell students to make two or three columns with their syllables on their desks or on the floor.

3. Have students take turns being the teacher.
    -   The teacher puts out three word parts, one from each column.
    -   The student segments and blends the word.
    -   The teacher makes a change in one part of the word at the oral level.
    -   The student takes out one chunk and replaces it with the correct word part to form the new word.
    -   Circulate among the pairs and listen to the students read their words and support them as they make changes.

Stretching Students' Learning

-   Use increasingly complex words, syllable patterns, and morphemes for sound mapping.

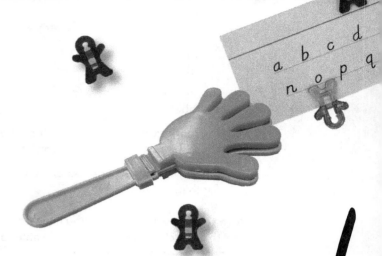

Clothespin Phonics

Activity Overview

Clothespin Phonics is a simple and engaging activity that develops and reinforces students' skills in identifying and matching sounds with the letter or letters that make those sounds. Being able to quickly connect sounds to graphemes is necessary for success in reading and spelling.

Materials • • • • •

- ◉ Alphabet or grapheme strips
- ◉ Simple pictures (or objects)
- ◉ Clothespins (colored clothespins— green, yellow, and red—*optional*)
- ◉ Student whiteboards, dry-erase markers, and erasers
- ◉ Magnetic letters and boards
- ◉ Two word lists (five words per list)

Whole Classroom Instruction

Set the purpose. Say: "In this activity, you will be listening for certain sounds in words and then matching them to the letters that represent those sounds. Being able to hear sounds and quickly recognize the letters that stand for those sounds will help you to become good readers and spellers."

You can use colored clothespins, if you can find them: green—beginning sound (green means go), yellow—middle sound (yellow means caution), and red—ending sound (red means stop).

1. Give each student an alphabet strip or a more limited strip with specifically selected graphemes on it (for example, short vowels, digraphs, etc.) and clothespins.

2. Hold up a picture and say the name of the object shown, for instance, "pot." Tap out the sounds for added support. Explain that the initial sound in the word *pot* is /p/.

3. Have students say the word *pot*, and make sure they understand the meaning.

4. Model by saying, "The first sound in *pot* is /p/, so I will take my clothespin and place it over the *p*."

5. Ask students to take one of their clothespins and place it over the *p* on their alphabet strip.

6. Have the class say the word *pot* again, and this time listen for the final sound. Tap out the word together to isolate the sounds. See if someone can come up with the final sound. Put a clothespin over the *t*. Have the class follow along and do it with you.

7. Now, depending on the level of the students, you may ask who can hear the middle sound in *pot*. Tap again to help everyone hear it. Emphasize the /ŏ/ sound as you get to the middle

tap. Ask the students to follow you and put a clothespin over the middle sound on their alphabet strip.

8. Instruct students to look at their clothespins and write the word *pot* on their whiteboards. Once they have written the word, they will touch and say the word chorally.

9. Repeat this activity with other pictures (or with words presented orally, if students are ready for that).

Return to the purpose. Say: "You have been working on connecting sounds in words with the letters that match those sounds. Being able to put sounds and letters together quickly will help you to be good readers and spellers."

Small Group Work

Students will continue to work on the same concept of rapid connection and recognition of sounds and letters; however, this time they will be touching the letter sound you call out.

1. Give small magnetic boards with magnetic letters to students.

2. Select the graphemes that will be the focus of instruction and arrange the magnetic letters in alphabetical order on a magnetic board.

3. Point to a letter, and ask a student to make the correct sound. If the student responds correctly, that means the student can express the correct sound when he sees the letter (expressive practice).

4. Say a sound and ask the same student to point to the correct letter. If the student responds correctly, that means he can recognize the sound when he hears it and can match it to the letter or letters that stand for that sound (receptive practice). Repeat with other students in the small group.

5. Say a word and tell the students to find the correct letters and build the word on their boards.
   - ☙ Have students segment and blend the word.
   - ☙ Tell students to change the word (one change at a time): the initial, middle, or ending sound (for example, *sap* to *tap*, *stamp* to *stomp*). Have them make 10 changes.

6. Choose a few of the words that were part of the chain, and ask the students to use them in sentences.

Independent Practice

Repeat this activity with students working in pairs. Partners will take turns being the "teacher" and the "student."

1. Give partners alphabet strips, clothespins, and two lists of five words each.

2. Explain that the "teacher" will give the "student" the first word on their list and that both will tap out the word together.

3. Tell the "student" to put a clothespin on the first sound, the second, and finally the final sound, of their alphabet strip.

4. Have both the "teacher" and the "student" write the word on their whiteboards, being sure to include beginning, middle, and ending sounds.

5. Instruct students to switch roles and repeat the activity.

Stretching Students' Learning

- ◎ Use more difficult phonics concepts, such as syllable and morphemes.

- ◎ This activity can be scaffolded up to work with multisyllabic words by having students put syllables in a line using a syllable strip.

Example:

Multisyllabic word = **transportation**
Have students:

1. Put a clothespin next to the syllable *trans*.

2. Then, put two clothespins next to the syllables *por* and *ta*.

3. Finally, put a clothespin next to the syllable *tion*.

4. Write the whole word on the board.

5. Have students draw a line for each clothespin (syllable) on a whiteboard.

6. Say the word and copy the syllables: *trans por ta tion*.

Where Is the Sound?

Activity Overview

Good readers can rapidly and automatically sound out new words they encounter. They have a clear understanding of the alphabetic principle and use their sound/symbol knowledge read new words. Where Is the Sound? gives students opportunities to sound out words using words that have the same letters but in different positions. It reinforces sound/symbol knowledge and provides repetition that will help students work toward mastery and automaticity in applying their alphabetic knowledge.

Materials

- Letter cards (see Appendix B)
- Student whiteboards, dry-erase markers, and erasers
- Speed Drill Worksheet (see Appendix A)
- Timers (*optional*)
- Pictures (*optional*)
- File folders and sticky notes
- Stickers (stars or hearts)

Whole Classroom Instruction

Set the purpose. Say: "You will be practicing sounding out words. Reading words that have the sounds in different parts of the word, such as the beginning, the middle, or the end, will help you to be better at reading words that you have never seen before."

Where Is the Sound? is similar to the Physical Phonics activity; however, the intent is to change the position of the sounds within words so that students can practice the same sounds in different positions.

1. Distribute letter cards.

2. Call up a group of four students with predetermined letter cards, for example, the students who have the letters *t, n, y, s*, and *t.*

3. Ask the group standing in the front of the room to make the word *nut.*

4. Tell the students at their desks to write the word *nut* on their whiteboards, touch and say the word *nut*, and then read it again, blending the sounds and reading it smoothly.

5. Briefly discuss the meaning of the word.

6. Now, ask the group at the front to make the word *sun.*

7. Tell the students at their desks to write the word *sun*, touch and say the word *sun*, and then read it again, recoding the sounds and reading it smoothly.

8. Briefly discuss the meaning of the word.

9. Next, ask the group at the front to make the word *stunt*.

10. Again, tell the students seated to make the change and read the word.

11. Repeat the activity with different letters, such as *sh*, *m*, *a*, *i*, *ng*, and *d*, and ask students to create *ship*, *mash*, and *dashing*.

Return to the purpose. Say: "You have been practicing reading words with the same sounds but in different parts of the word. This kind of practice will help you to recognize and read sounds wherever they are located in words."

Small Group Work

1. Show students a list of words on chart paper or a whiteboard to read with sounds in various positions.

2. Dictate a list of words to spell and read, such as *thank*, *math*, and *brother,* or, if students are ready, *withhold*, *thinking*, and *mathematics*.

This student places a sticker over the target concept.

3. Have students write the words, then place a sticker over the part of the word that is the target of the instruction.

4. Distribute a Speed Drill Worksheet to the group and conduct a drill of words that use sounds flexibly, similar to the examples given in whole class instruction.

    ☺ Place five words in a fifty- or one hundred-word speed drill grid, randomly repeating the words. Using a timer, see how many words the group (or individual students) can read correctly in 1 minute. Place a slash mark at the end of 1 minute and count the number of words read accurately. Repeat for another minute. Chart any progress.

5. Discuss the words students have been working with, being sure that students can create sentences and make connections to their background knowledge.

Independent Practice

Have students work in pairs for this variation of the activity. The pairs will take turns being the "student" and the "teacher." Give each student pair a folder that has sticky notes with letters written on them placed across the top half of the folder.

1. Give partners a list of simple words with the following four consonant-vowel patterns: CVC (*cub*), CVCC (*camp*), CCVC (*stop*), and CCVCC (*stomp*).

2. Explain that the "teacher" will read a word and the "student," using the folders and sticky notes, will build the word, touch each sound, and then blend the sounds reading each word. Next the "student" will write the words on a piece of paper and create one sentence using at least two of the words. For example, *can*, *math*, *that*, and *think* = I hope **that** you **can** help me with **math**.

3. Have students switch roles and repeat the activity.

    ☺ If appropriate, give partners timers and have them time each other on speed drills using the sounds they have been practicing. They can work on speeding up their ability to read the words more quickly.

Phonics *Where Is the Sound?*

Flip Over Sounds

Activity Overview

Flip Over Sounds gives students opportunities to build and read words using movable letters. Word building involves the core phonological skill of blending and segmenting sounds as well as the skill of manipulating sounds. This activity strengthens the phonological processor while reinforcing sound/symbol and orthographic knowledge, leading to mastery and automaticity in those areas. While working on word building with your students, emphasize vocabulary, background building, and contextual understanding of the words being built.

Materials

- Letter cards mounted on green, yellow, and red construction paper
- Three baskets to hold the letter cards
- Dice
- Student whiteboards, dry-erase markers, and erasers
- File folders and sticky notes
- Index cards that match the letter cards
- Pictures (*optional*)

Whole Classroom Instruction

Set the purpose. Say: "This activity will give you a chance to build words by practicing what you already know about letters and sound. As you practice word building, reading, spelling, and writing will get easier."

Sort the letter cards into three baskets, as you did in the I'm Magic *e* activity:

- First basket: beginning consonants, digraphs, and initial blends (depending on what has already been taught) mounted on green paper.

- Middle basket: vowels or vowel teams mounted on yellow paper.

- Third basket: ending consonants, digraphs, and ending blends mounted on red paper.

1. Choose three students to stand behind the baskets and explain that they will be building real or nonsense words.

2. Students at their desks are engaged throughout the activity because they are using whiteboards, markers, and erasers to track the changes and read the changes, both in front of the room and then again on their whiteboards.

3. Ask each student to take the top letter card out of their basket. One at a time, have each student say the sound they are holding and then blend all three sounds to make a word.

4. Call on different students at their desks to roll the die. The number rolled dictates which student at the front of the room will put the card she is holding face down next to the basket and draw a new letter card (see the following Flip Over Sounds Rules). After the student

has drawn a new card, the other two students will once again segment and blend the three sounds and create a new word.

Flip Over Sounds Rules

The initial created word = **shop**.*

- ◉ Roll 1. The initial sound gets changed—**shop** changes to **mop**.

- ◉ Roll 2. The vowel gets changed—**mop** changes to **map**.

- ◉ Roll 3. The ending sound gets changed—**map** changes to **mat**.

- ◉ Roll 4. Free Choice: The roller chooses someone else in the class who gets to decide which sound changes—**mat** changes to **chat**.

- ◉ Roll 5. The vowel and final sound both change—**chat** changes to **chop**.

- ◉ Roll 6. All sounds change—**chop** changes to **pet**.

*This example uses changes that are all real words; it is likely that you may go back and forth between real and make-believe words.

Return to the Purpose. Say: "You've been building words, using what you already know about letters and sounds. As you practice word building, reading, spelling, and writing will get easier."

Small Group Work

In this variation of Flip Over Sounds, students participate in a folder activity that reinforces the same word-building concept that was introduced to the whole class.

1. Distribute folders, sticky notes, and blank paper to each student in the group.

2. Tell students to create three columns on the top half of their folder labeled "Beginning," "Middle," and "Ending."

3. Demonstrate for students by writing some beginning, middle, and ending sounds on sticky notes. Place three of the sticky notes on which you have written sounds on the bottom half of a folder, creating a word (e.g., *cat*). Segment and blend the word.

4. Have students, as a group, write some beginning, middle, and ending sounds on sticky notes. Place the sticky notes under the columns labeled "Beginning," "Middle," and "Ending."

   ↻ Ask if someone can find a word among the sticky notes.

   ↻ Build that word on the bottom half of the folder and copy it onto a piece of paper.

5. Instruct students to use some of the words in a sentence orally and then write a sentence on their paper using the word (this can be the same sentence or different). For example, "The **cat can lap** the milk.

6. Have students take turns building as many words as they can with sticky notes on the bottom half of their own folder, using all the sounds, and then individually recording them on their paper.

   ↻ If time permits, ask them to write a sentence for several of the words on their paper.

   ↻ After students have created and recorded a word, they place the sticky notes back on the top half of their folder to be used again to form a new word.

Independent Practice

In this variation of Flip Over Sounds, students work with a partner, keeping track of words and recording them as they do the activity.

1. Give each pair of students dice, Flip Over Sounds Rules, and small decks of index cards that match the basket cards (beginning/middle/ending).

2. Have students arrange the cards in three stacks (beginning, middle, ending) then take turns rolling the die and making a change by turning over a beginning, middle, or ending card according to the rules for creating new words.

3. Have students make a sentence for each real word they create.

Stretching Students' Learning

⊚   Fill the baskets with syllables, prefixes, roots, and suffixes if the students have already had instruction in those phonics concepts.

Walkabout Words

Activity Overview

Walkabout Words is an activity that reinforces phonics and morphological concepts that have been previously learned. It allows students to think about and analyze phonics concepts as they move about the room, looking for other students who hold word parts with which they can build a multisyllabic word that you provide from content-area selections. Students at their seats apply meta-linguistic skills by comparing and contrasting their own work with that done by the students involved with the actual, physical word-building activities.

Materials • • • • • •

- ◉ Index cards with word parts written on them
- ◉ Student whiteboards, colored dry-erase markers, and erasers
- ◉ Sticky notes and file folders
- ◉ Picture cards (*optional*)

Whole Classroom Instruction

Set the purpose. Say: "This activity will give you practice building words using word parts you already know. Understanding and recognizing word parts will help you to read big words more easily."

Choose word parts, based on previously learned phonics or morphological concepts, and write them on index cards. Use content area multisyllabic words or words from grade-level stories or passages. For example, if the class has been learning about desert habitats, you might use the following word parts: /liz/ /ard/   /rep/ /tile/   /des/ /ert/   /cac/ /tus/

1. Distribute the cards to the whole class (or to part of the class).

2. Have all students with word part cards walk around the room, holding their card in front of them so others can see it.

3. Tell students to look for a word part that will help them complete a whole multisyllabic word. When they find a match that makes a complete word, they should stop and stand with the person holding the matching card and become partners.

4. After everyone is matched, have the student pairs take turns reading their words so the whole class gets the benefit of hearing all the words.

   ↺ Record the words on the board so the entire class can benefit from everyone's efforts (and to use later during independent practice).

   ↺ On the walls around the room, tape pieces of cardstock with one syllable type listed on each (open, closed, silent *e*, r-controlled, consonant + *le*, vowel pair). Ask students to move to the sign that represents their syllable. If you have taught only two or three types of syllables, then only sort for those syllable types.

Return to the purpose. Say:
"You've been building words based on word parts you already know. When you can recognize word parts and build words with them, reading big words will become easier."

Small Group Work

1. Place a stack of word part cards on the desk and ask the students to sort for word parts that, when combined, form a new word. Students may find more than one word that can be made. This activity can also be done around a theme being studied, such as using desert words (/des/ /ert/, /rep/ /tile, /me/ /sa/, /in/ /sect/, etc.), content area words, or words that demonstrate the use of a particular phonics concept, syllable type, or morphological unit that has been taught.

    ☻ At a more advanced level, multisyllabic words like the following could be formed:
    /trans/ /form/   /trans/ /fer/   /trans/ /form/ /a/ /tion/

2. Have students turn to their neighbors and use two of the words they have built in sentences, trying to make sentences that relate to their own lives. Ask each student to share one sentence aloud with the group.

3. Next, ask students to choose one of the sentences and write it on their whiteboards. Have them each select a colored marker and put a box around the target words built (coding for the target words).

Independent Practice

For repeated practice, students will work in pairs using the words you recorded on the board during whole class instruction.

1. Distribute sticky notes and file folders to everyone.

2. Ask students to write in their Word Work Notebooks the words recorded earlier on the board. Tell them to then deconstruct the words, writing word parts on sticky notes and placing the sticky notes on the top part of the folder in mixed-up order.

3. Have partners exchange folders and, using the mixed-up sticky notes, form 10 words correctly on the bottom half of the folder.

4. Ask partners to read their words to each other and then choose two to use in sentences. The students will tell each other their sentences and then write the sentences in their notebooks.

Stretching Students' Learning

    ☻ Use increasingly complex words, syllable patterns, and morphemes for word building.

Fluency Activities

21. Phrase Reading
22. Reading Buddies
23. Alphabetic Prosody
24. Read With Speed
25. Triplet Reading
26. Ready, Set, Say It
27. Wear a Word
28. Words by Heart
29. Flyswatter Syllables
30. Schoolwide Reading

R eading fluency refers to the ability to read accurately and at a minimal rate, with expression and deep understanding (Hudson, Mercer, & Lane, 2000). Getting students "up to speed" means that they become automatic with the underlying subskills of reading, namely phonemic awareness, phonics, and vocabulary. When students master these basic skills, they will be free to address issues of comprehension. Students need enough opportunities to practice basic skills so that they move from accurate to automatic. All the activities in this book are in some way related to fluency in that they are designed to give students extra opportunities to master reading skills. The fluency activities in this section focus specifically on word-, phrase-, sentence-, and passage-level fluency, in addition to developing automaticity with punctuation, which increases prosodic fluency (expression).

The Four Processing Systems Connection

For students to reach the level of fluent reading, they must be able to read easily enough that they have enough attention left over to focus on comprehending what they are reading. Fluent readers are not merely fast readers; they are readers who read with expression and understanding.

Fluent reading depends on the automatic processing of sounds and symbols (involving the phonological processor and the orthographic processor). Vocabulary knowledge, in which meanings are easily recalled (the meaning processor), is also essential. Finally the ability to link the known words to background knowledge is necessary for fluent decoding and comprehension. All of the four processors are involved in this section's activities. When the four processors are working with ease and automaticity, students become fluent readers.

The LETRS Connection

◎ *Language Essentials for Teachers of Reading and Spelling* (LETRS), Module 5 — *Getting Up to Speed: Developing Fluency.*

Fluency Activities

The Assessment Connection

◎ *DIBELS: Dynamic Indicators of Basic Early Literacy Skills.* Oral Reading Fluency: Measures whether the student can read connected text accurately and fluently.

◎ *DIBELS: Dynamic Indicators of Basic Early Literacy Skills.* Nonsense Word Fluency: Measures whether students can: (1) name letter sounds and (2) blend sounds to read unfamiliar words with short vowels in consonant-vowel-consonant or vowel-consonant syllable patterns.

◎ The *Test of Word Reading Efficiency* (TOWRE) is a nationally normed measure of word reading accuracy and fluency.

◎ The *Test of Silent Word Reading Fluency* (TOSWRF) measures a student's ability to recognize printed words accurately and efficiently.

◎ The *Test of Silent Contextual Reading Fluency* (TOSCRF) is a quick and accurate method of assessing the silent general reading ability of students ranging in age from 7 years, 0 months to 18 years, 11 months.

The ELL Connection

Many of the activities in this section will be effective with ELLs without any alteration. However, a few small changes can have a great impact on the achievement and skill development for these students. The following are a few ideas to try that may enhance the effectiveness of the fluency activities:

◎ Make sure that the content of words, phrases, and sentences used for building fluency at the basic building-block levels are within the linguistic background knowledge level of the students.

◎ Phrase-cue reading can be particularly helpful in increasing comprehension because it reduces longer, more difficult sentences into sentence chunks that can be more easily read and understood.

◎ Having students illustrate in a short and simple manner the meaning of words, phrases, and sentences can help check comprehension.

◎ Prosody is an important reflection of comprehension in all languages. Prosody activities translate well into the students' primary languages, as well.

◎ Repeated reading is an excellent way for ELLs to hear the flow and rhythm of the new language. Reading a passage to students for the first time may add to their understanding of the passage.

◎ Scaffold repeated reading activities by having students read chorally until they are comfortable enough to read individually.

◎ Improve fluency by previewing content and vocabulary carefully. Select material that has accompanying pictures to help build background.

◎ Speed drills can give students opportunities for extra practice after direct instruction in the concepts of the code. Sometimes students who have been transitioned into English-only instruction in second, third, or fourth grade have missed opportunities for direct instruction in the code, and that knowledge is primarily assumed.

Fluency

Dig In to Learn More

Adams, G., & Brown, S. (2007). *The six-minute solution: 2007. A reading fluency program, grades K–8* (2006). Longmont, CO: Sopris West Educational Services.

Beck. R., Conrad D., & Anderson, P. (1997). *Basic skill builders*. Longmont, CO: Sopris West Educational Services.

Foorman, B., Fletcher, J., & Francis, D. (1997). *A scientific approach to reading instruction.* Learning Disabilities Online. Available at: http:www.ldonline.org/ld_indepth/reading/cars.html

Moats, L. C. (2005). *Language essentials for teachers of reading and spelling (LETRS). Module 5—Getting Up to Speed: Developing Fluency.* Longmont, CO: Sopris West Educational Services.

Wolf, M. (2001). *Dyslexia, fluency, and the brain.* Baltimore, MD: York Press.

Fluency Activities

Phrase Reading

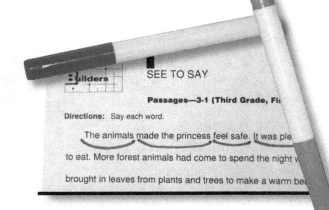

Activity Overview

When students have difficulty with phrase reading, often the problem has roots in oral language. At the oral level, it is easy to begin supporting students' learning by using your voice to cue students as to where the phrases are. This develops the awareness of phrasing so that when students go to the text, they are more sensitive to the phrases in the sentences.

Phrase reading builds a bridge between word-by-word reading and connected text reading. Phrases carry meaning, so proficient phrase reading leads to increased reading comprehension and increased expression. Phrase-cue reading strategies help the dysfluent reader begin to notice the phrases in text. This Phrase Reading activity gives you strategies for instruction at the phrase level, helping students to take a more complex sentence and "code" it for phrase chunks.

Materials ● ● ● ● ● ●

- ◎ Plastic hand clappers (*optional*)*
- ◎ Whiteboard, dry-erase markers, and eraser
- ◎ Overhead projector, transparency, and pen
- ◎ Student whiteboards, dry-erase markers, and erasers
- ◎ Folded paper (three columns) with a sentence from students' text in first column
- ◎ Koosh ball*
- ◎ Strips of paper and scissors
- ◎ Reading books at students' independent reading level

* Available in the optional Classroom Manipulatives Kit

Whole Classroom Instruction

Set the purpose. Say: "Phrases carry the meaning in sentences. Being able to see where the phrases start and stop will help you to read more fluently and improve your reading comprehension. This activity will give you practice identifying where phrases are in sentences."

1. Distribute plastic hand clappers to everyone, if available.

2. Model the process of phrase-cue marking.
   - ℮ Begin with a single sentence, using the whiteboard, marking the phrases first by placing a large dot or a forward slash between the phrases: **The boy likes to hike • with his dog.** (Or, **The boy likes to hike / with his dog.**)
   - ℮ Using a marker of another color, "scoop" under the phrases.
   - ℮ Repeat this procedure with another sentence, first placing a dot between the phrases and then scooping under the phrases.
   - ℮ Using the overhead projector, write a sentence on a transparency. It could be taken from the text students are reading. Make sure it is at an appropriate reading level.
   - ℮ Ask students to copy the sentence onto their whiteboards.

3. Have students scoop the phrases in their sentence.

    ☞ Ask for a student volunteer to come up to the overhead projector, first separating the phrases with a dot and then scooping under the phrases with another colored marker.

    ☞ Tell students seated at their desks to compare what they scooped to the overhead model. If they agree with the overhead model, they can clap their hand clappers (or clap their hands or put thumbs up or thumbs down).

    ☞ Repeat this process three times.

Return to the purpose. Say: "You have been practicing identifying where the phrases are in sentences. Becoming good at identifying phrases will help you read and comprehend better."

Small Group Work

1. Give students paper that has been folded into three columns. In the first column there should be a sentence from their text. Depending on the level of your students, you can either write a sentence in the first column and make copies for the group or write a sentence on the whiteboard or chart paper and have students copy it in the first column.

2. Working together, have students read the sentence as a group in the first column, scoop the phrases, and reread the sentence with the correct phrase prosody.

3. Instruct students to write the individual phrases in the two remaining columns.

The boy likes to hike • with his dog.	The boy likes to hike	with his dog.
Can you come • to my birthday party?	Can you come	to my birthday party?

Talking Classroom

4. Model saying a two-phrase sentence orally and ask students to repeat it. "Can you come to my birthday party?"

    ☞ Next, toss a Koosh ball to one of the students, repeat the sentence, and ask the student to listen for and repeat the first phrase. "Can you come"

    ☞ After the student repeats the phrase, have that student throw the Koosh ball back to you.

    ☞ Repeat the process with the second phrase of the sentence. Throw the ball to another student, who should repeat the first phrase and then add the second phrase.

    ☞ Practicing phrasing at the oral level can help students internalize the concept of phrases so that they can better identify them in their reading and read with better expression and comprehension.

Independent Practice

Students will work independently and then finish the activity with a partner.

1. Give students strips of paper and scissors.

2. Have them copy a sentence from their reading book onto the strip.

3. Tell them to scoop the phrases and then cut the sentence into the scooped phrases.

Fluency *Phrase Reading*

4. Next, have students reconstruct the sentence, then write it on another piece of paper.

5. Have students repeat this process three times.

6. Ask students to exchange their cut phrase strips with their partner and to each reconstruct the sentences made by their partners, reading the sentences aloud.

Stretching Students' Learning

◉   Students can create sentences and divide them into phrases by underlining the phrases.

Reading Buddies

Activity Overview

Reading Buddies is an activity that helps build fluency with connected text. Fluency is the bridge to comprehension. A critical goal in reading fluency instruction is getting students up to a minimal rate necessary to facilitate comprehension. However, rate alone is not the goal of fluency instruction. The goal is for students to get "up to speed" so that they read with enough ease that their attention can be devoted to comprehending the text.

Materials

- Books at students' independent reading level
- Class list with students' reading assessment information

Reading Buddies provides an opportunity for students to read passages with their peers instead of reading independently. While sustained silent reading is a popular approach for independent reading practice, it poses several challenges for growth in the struggling reader. Struggling readers often have difficulty attending to the text during the reading period. Further, if the students have self-selected books that are too difficult for them to read and they have misunderstandings about the code of the English language, they will be practicing errors without feedback and error correction. Reading Buddies helps to ensure that the students will be attending to the text and reading words out loud. If the partnering is done carefully, then the student can also get some level of corrective feedback and have opportunities for sharing and responding to content-enhancing comprehension through the oral dialog.

Whole Classroom Instruction

Set the purpose. Say: "This activity will give you practice reading aloud with a partner and sharing what you have read. When you can read with a buddy, you will be more likely to be able to stay focused and give each other help and feedback when something is hard."

1. Have students sit next to their assigned buddy.

2. Use a text or story that the class has practiced or that is familiar.

3. Tell Reader #1 to read a section—a page or a paragraph.
   - Emphasize the importance of comfortable speed, reading with expression, and understanding what is read.

4. Explain that Reader #2 will pick up reading when Reader #1 stops reading.

5. Direct students to go back and question each other about what they read after the reading is finished: "What was this part about?"

Determining Reading Buddies*

1. Select passages in selected books that can be read with 95 percent accuracy.

2. Rank the class according to reading ability (based on assessment information).

3. Divide the class list in half.

4. Assign pairs by matching the top reader of the top half of the class with the top reader of the bottom half of the class, and so forth. (Reader #1 is the stronger reader and should read first while Reader #2 listens and follows the text.) These pairings are likely to be close enough in reading ability that they can work well together. Check the pairings and make changes to buddy arrangements that might not be compatible as students work together over time.

    ☺ Be careful about peer assignments for children with exceptional needs, for example, highly gifted readers or children with learning disabilities or emotional handicaps. Make a plan for those students who need a more individualized program during this time.

    ☺ Children with attentional weaknesses may need to be close to you during this period of time.

    *This method of determining reading buddies comes from the guidelines in P. Mathes (2001), *PALS (Peer-Assisted Learning Strategies)*, Longmont, CO: Sopris West Educational Services.

6. Reinforce appropriate behavior by keeping lists of books read and giving points for following and listening well. The success of this activity will depend on teaching and reinforcing the behaviors you expect. Using whatever behavior management system you prefer throughout the school day will be the most effective.

7. Ask each buddy pair to share with another buddy pair what they read about.

Return to the purpose. Say: "We have reading buddies to increase our reading skills and to have fun reading together."

Stretching Students' Learning

This activity is easily scaffolded for gifted readers. Gifted readers are often asked to read alone, but they enjoy reading aloud and sharing just as much as able readers. Allowing them to read at a more advanced level but still have opportunities to share is important. Using literature as well as nonfiction that can be used for research-based projects works well.

Alphabetic Prosody

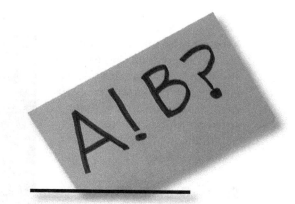

Activity Overview

One definition of reading fluency is "accurate reading at a minimal rate with appropriate prosodic features (expression)" (Hudson, Mercer, & Lane, 2000). Prosodic features refer to punctuation and phrasing. Fluent readers read in phrases, using the intonation and prosodic features of the text, therefore reading with appropriate expression.

Automaticity occurs when a skill is performed so easily that it is done without conscious attention. Alphabetic Prosody is an activity that can help students learn to pay attention to punctuation marks and understand what they represent, rapidly and automatically. Once students have mastered the meaning of the punctuation marks, they can transfer that automatic knowledge to sentences and connected text quite easily.

Materials

- Card stock printed with single letters of the alphabet
- Marker
- Plastic sheet protectors
- Student whiteboards, dry-erase markers, and erasers

Whole Classroom Instruction

Set the purpose. Say: "Paying attention to punctuation marks will help you to read with expression. When you read with expression, it is a sign that you understand what you are reading. This activity will give you practice reading punctuation marks."

Prior to the activity, take the card stock printed with single letters and punctuate the letters with punctuation that has been previously taught, for example, **A! A? A.** Place the letter cards in plastic sheet protectors and arrange in alphabetical order.

1. Remind students what an exclamation mark means and how to read it when they encounter one.

2. Read the letters **A!, B!,** and **C!** to the class with a lot of excitement.

3. Ask the class to say the next two or three letters with you: "**D!, E!, F!,** and **G!**"

4. Ask the class to read the next set of letters in unison without you: "**H!, I!, J!, K!**"

5. Repeat this activity with other graphemes and add other punctuation marks (like question marks and periods) that have been taught.

Return to the purpose. Say:
"You've been practicing paying attention to punctuation marks. Punctuation marks will help you to read with expression. When you read with expression, it is a sign that you understand what you are reading."

Small Group Work

1. Say a sound and ask students to write the letter(s) (grapheme) for that sound on their whiteboards.

2. Repeat the sound in an excited way and ask students to add the punctuation mark after the letter(s) that makes the reader know it needs to be read in an excited manner.

3. Have students say the sound with expression as they write it and then again when they are finished writing the exclamation mark.

4. Say several sounds with excitement and ask students to write the letter(s) and use the correct punctuation mark. For instance, say "/sh!/" and have students write **sh!**

5. Repeat this process with other punctuation marks that students have been taught.

6. Give the group a simple sentence to copy onto their whiteboards. For example: **The dog barked.**

   ᴗ Have them read it as a simple declarative sentence with a period at the end: **"The dog barked."**

   ᴗ Then ask them to change the period to a question mark and read the sentence again: **"The dog barked?"**

   ᴗ Finally, have them change the question mark to an exclamation mark and read it in an excited manner: **"The dog barked!"**

Independent Practice

Alphabetic Prosody can be repeated with students working in pairs.

1. Have each partner write out the first eight letters of the alphabet on their whiteboard and put punctuation marks in between the letters. Examples: **A, B, C, D. E! F! G? H.**

2. Ask the partners to take turns reading each other's alphabet. Students can repeat this step with another set of alphabet letters or with the entire alphabet if time allows.

3. Next, tell the partners to work together to choose simple words and phrases with different punctuation marks and to write them on their whiteboards. When they finish writing, have them read the words and phrases aloud together: **"Dog! Dog? Dog."**

Stretching Students' Learning

◉ Students can practice Alphabetic Prosody using sentences and short passages they create themselves. They can share them with another student and read each other's punctuation marks.

Read With Speed

Activity Overview

Read With Speed presents speed drills to help students build automaticity with individual concepts that can then be applied within the context of text reading. The drills allow students to practice a skill out of the context of connected text, which requires attention to decoding, sight words, and comprehension of the whole text. Doing some practice out of the context of the text allows students to devote more attention to processing letter/sounds, orthographic or morphemic patterns, vocabulary words, and other phonics concepts. Speed reading at the word level increases reading comprehension (Foorman, Fletcher, & Francis, 1997). Speed drills help students build correct models in their brains, leading to more automatic access of the model during text reading. Word fluency levels develop first, before phrasing and passage fluency. When students "overlearn" a word or concept, it becomes so automatic that it requires no conscious thought, therefore allowing for attention to be devoted to comprehension.

Materials • • • • • •

- Overhead projector
- Transparencies of prepared speed drills (*Skill Builders* is available through Sopris West; *Concept Phonics* is available through Oxton House Publishing)
- Stopwatch
- Student whiteboards, dry-erase markers, and erasers
- Speed Drill Worksheet (see Appendix A)
- Pictures and objects (*optional*)

Whole Classroom Instruction

Set the purpose. Say: "In this activity, you will be practicing speed drills to help you become more automatic with reading skills you already know. When reading skills are automatic, you will be able to pay more attention to understanding what you are reading instead of just figuring out what the words are."

Speed drills are done primarily at the small group and paired level. However, they can be introduced as a whole class activity and practiced at this level so that you can then release students to work in pairs or with para-educators, parents, or peer tutors for individual work.

1. Use an overhead projector and put up a prepared speed drill transparency with whatever concept you are working on with the class:
   - High-frequency words (*that, what, there, where, though*)
   - Words that demonstrate a phonics concept (*mat, hip, hop, cut, dig*)
   - Orthographic patterns (*light, sight, fight, bright*)

    ↺ Letter-naming fluency (*k, m, r, b, f*)

    ↺ Words that demonstrate a morphologic concept (*transform, reform, deform, inform, platform*)

2. An example of a short vowel speed drill follows. To do the speed drill, place five words in a fifty- or one hundred-word speed drill grid, randomly repeating the words. Using a timer, see how many words the group (or individual students) can read correctly in 1 minute. Place a slash mark at the end of 1 minute and count the number of words read accurately. Repeat for another minute. Chart any progress.

mat	dog	cut	pin	pen
dog	pen	mat	cut	pin
cut	pin	pen	dog	mat

Return to the Purpose. Say: "You are getting faster at reading these words. When you can read these words faster, you will be able to pay more attention to understand what you're reading."

Small Group Work

1. Working with a speed drill on the same concept as you did with the whole class, hold a prepared speed drill up so that students can see the words.

2. Set a stopwatch and let students chorally read the words and see how long it takes them to read through the speed drill.

3. Using the same speed drill, have students take turns reading the words aloud.

4. For the third reading of the speed drill, use a stopwatch again and have students read the words chorally and see if they have reduced their time for completing the speed drill.

5. Using their whiteboards, have students map words that include the target skill and/or write sentences that include the skill that has been emphasized in the speed drill. Examples:

    ↺ Make a list of short vowel words, such as *map, cat, fin, fish, cub, tub, shop, pot, pet,* and *hen.*

The teacher points to words during a small group speed drill activity.

    ↺ Model tapping the sounds in the word *shop*: "/ sh/ /o/ /p/."

    ↺ Ask questions about the word: "What is the first sound?" (/sh/) "What is the last sound?" (/p/) "What is the vowel in the middle?" (/ŏ/)

    ↺ Draw lines for each sound in the word. Shop = ___ ___ ___.

    ↺ Tap out the sounds again and fill in the sounds one tap at a time = **<u>sh</u> <u>o</u> <u>p</u>**.

    ↺ Draw a heart over the vowel in the middle to draw attention to the important and sometimes tricky part of the word that students will need to learn "by heart."

    ↺ Ask students to write a sentence using the word. For example, "I go with my mom to **shop** for food."

6. Ask students to turn to their neighbor and use one of the words they have been working with in a sentence, making a personal connection if possible.

Independent Practice

The focus of this activity is to practice a pretaught concept. This strategy can be very effective in moving a concept from accurate (but slow) to accurate and automatic.

Have students work together in pairs or independently with a para-professional or another student. If students are working with other students, they should be paired with a student who can read the words correctly. Because there are only five words on the speed drills, you can check on students' ability to read the words accurately.

1. Tell students to work for 3 minutes on a teacher-prepared speed drill activity (three timed repetitions).

2. Ask students to chart their progress on their word-reading fluency.

Stretching Students' Learning

◎ This activity can be done with simple to more complex phonics concepts and sight words, syllables types, or morphemes in which students have already had direct instruction.

Triplet Reading

Activity Overview

Triplet Reading builds fluency with connected text. Fluency is the bridge to comprehension. A critical goal in reading-fluency instruction is to get students up to a minimal rate necessary to facilitate comprehension. Triplet Reading provides a strategy that allows students to improve their reading rate of short passages by reading the passages three times. In addition, the students will be measuring and charting changes and growth in their reading fluency over the course of three separate opportunities. Charting their progress enables students to note how their fluency skills are developing.

Materials

- Teacher prepared transparency of short passages at students' reading level
- Overhead projector
- Timers
- Charting sheet
- Short passages at students' reading level placed in plastic sheet protectors
- Whisper phones*
- Dry-erase markers and erasers

* Available in the optional Classroom Manipulatives Kit

Charting Fluency Data

Advantages of charting fluency progress are:

- Small gains are visible.

- Steady growth over time is visible.

- Students are competing against themselves only.

- Teachers can tell if improvement is occurring and can change something if it is not.

- A clear benchmark is in sight.

The Mechanics of Charting

1. Decide on the duration of intervention (8–10 weeks).

2. Decide on the baseline word count per minute (WCPM) after giving students three passages at goal level (grade level).

3. Plot an "aim line" between the students' baseline and a suitable benchmark.

4. Plot weekly results of progress-monitoring assessment over that period.

5. Make a change to the reading passage used if there is no progress in three weeks.

Whole Classroom Instruction

Set the Purpose. Say: "When you can read a passage easily, you are more likely to understand what you have read. This activity will give you the opportunity to read a passage three times and chart your progress from a 'cold read,' when the words are new and unfamiliar, to a 'hot read,' when the words and ideas are familiar."

Fluency

Before beginning the activity, select a passage to read and preview new vocabulary and concepts that may be encountered in the passage. Begin with passages that can be read with 95 percent accuracy.

1. Put up a passage on an overhead projector.

2. Read the title of the passage. Mention something you know about from reading the title, and ask students to think about what they already know about the topic. This sets the purpose as comprehension rather than "fast reading."

3. Set a timer for 1 minute and have the class read aloud with you as you read the text for 1 minute.

4. Count all the words read in that minute.

5. Remove the passage from the overhead projector and put up a charting sheet. Show students how you can write the name of the passage, the date, and under the first column chart how many words correct per minute (WCPM) were read.

6. Ask the class to read the passage for a second time, this time silently together; do not time it or chart it.

7. When everyone has done their silent read of the passage, have the class read aloud once again, without your help. At the end of 1 minute, when the timer goes off, mark a bracket ( ]) where the reading stops.

8. Chart your third read and draw the class's attention to the fact that they have been able to read more words correct per minute the third time than the first.

Return to the purpose. Say: "You have been practicing reading the same passage three times. Your progress was charted from the first reading, when the words and ideas were new, to the third reading, when the words and ideas were familiar. When you can read a passage easily, you are more likely to understand what you have read."

Small Group Work

Before the activity, make copies of a passage that is at an appropriate level for the small group and place it in plastic sheet protectors.

1. Give each student:
   ℮ The passage in a plastic sheet protector
   ℮ A whisper phone
   ℮ A charting sheet with the name of the passage filled in

2. Using their markers, have students underline new vocabulary words that you have brought to their attention, if appropriate. Discuss the vocabulary.

3. Ask students to chorally read the passage along with you.

4. Tell each student to practice charting their words correct per minute on their charting sheet.

5. Have students whisper-read the passage using their whisper phones.

6. Instruct students to practice the passage a third time, charting their final WCPM to show improvement.

7. Ask students questions about the passage they have been reading. You can structure it with who, what, where, when, and why questions. This step is important because it reinforces that fluency practice is not about reading fast but about reading fast enough to understand.

Independent Practice

Select unfamiliar passages and place them in plastic sheet protectors. Have students work in pairs this time.

1. Give each student an unfamiliar passage, a charting sheet, and a whisper phone. Give each set of partners a timer.

2. Have all the students look for vocabulary words that they may not know and underline them with their markers.

3. Tell partners to take turns timing each other for their first 1-minute read.

4. Instruct students who were timed to chart how many words correct per minute they read.

5. Next, have partners read together chorally, using whisper phones for their second read.

6. Have partners take turns doing a third and final read, which they will chart once again.

7. Finally, tell partners to work together to create who, what, where, why, and when questions that relate to the passage they have read. (This can be done orally or in writing, depending on how much time you have for the activity.)

Ready, Set, Say It!

Activity Overview

Giving students the gift of repetition may be one of the most important strategies for building text fluency and comprehension. If working memory is filled up because students are trying to recall the meaning of a word or its pronunciation, comprehension may be compromised as the lack of automaticity leads to slower, less fluent reading.

Ready, Set, Say It! is an activity that provides opportunities for the review and practice of concepts that may have been learned but never automatized to allow for fluent reading. It provides teachers and students with an engaging structure in which to build the kind of practice necessary to move from accurate to automatic.

Materials

- Teacher prepared word cards
- Speed drill transparency showing the same words as on the word cards
- Overhead projector
- Timers
- Speed Drill Worksheet (see Appendix A)
- Student whiteboards, dry-erase markers, and erasers
- Charting sheet
- File folders and small sticky notes
- Picture cards (*optional*)

Whole Classroom Instruction

Set the purpose. Say: "This activity will give you practice reading words that contain certain word parts. Being able to quickly recognize word parts can make you a more fluent reader, and what you read will be easier to understand."

Based on the needs of your students, choose a concept or skill that you will work on, such as the word part *tion*. Make a set of cards containing words with *tion*: *nation, station, ration, caption, action, notion, fiction, mention, motion, friction, fraction, dictation, collection, education, inflation, segregation, integration.*

1. Divide the students into two teams and have the teams line up in front of you.

2. Say, "You are going to practice reading the word part *tion*. You have to learn to recognize it and remember that whenever you see it, you will pronounce it as 'shun,' even though it is spelled *t-i-o-n.*"

3. Hold up a word card for Team #1 first. Explain that the first student will get a chance to read the card in 1 second. If he can do it, then Team #1 scores a point. Team #2 will get a word next.

   ↻ As students attend to the words and practice reading silently as their team members read aloud, they will get a lot of extra practice with the concept.

4. Arrange a reward for the winning team, then have students take their seats.

5. Display an overhead transparency showing a speed drill that has the same words as the cards. Have the class review the concept by reading the words for 1 minute.

6. Count the number of words read in a minute.

Return to the purpose. Say: "You have been practicing reading words with certain word parts. Being able to quickly recognize word parts can make you become a more fluent reader. When you read fluently, what you read will be easier to understand."

Small Group Work

1. Working with a speed drill on the same concept as practiced with the whole class, hold up the speed drill so that students can see the words.

2. Set a count-down timer and let the students chorally read the words and see how long it takes them to read through the speed drill.

3. Holding up the same speed drill, have students take turns reading the words aloud.

4. For the third reading of the speed drill, use a timer again and have the students read the words chorally and see if they have reduced their time for completing the speed drill.

5. On their whiteboards, ask students to map words that use the target skill.
   - Mapping one-syllable words can be done by sound tapping and writing down each sound.
   - Mapping two-syllable words can be done by counting the syllables and drawing a line for each syllable, then tapping out the sounds in each syllable. If one of the syllables is a word part that is known automatically (like *tion*), it can be written without tapping the sounds. Remind students that *tion* is a part that they will need to learn by heart. (Therefore, *tion* is a "heart part.")

6. Give words such as *nation*.
   - First, have students count the syllables.
   - Next, ask them to draw two lines ___ ___.
   - Have them tap out the sounds in the first syllable and write them on the first line: **na.**
   - Now, tell students to write the second syllable on the second line, which is a heart part: **tion.**
   - Ask students to write a sentence using the pattern *tion*. For instance: I live in a big **nation.**

7. Ask students to turn to their neighbor and use one of the words you have been working with in a sentence, making a personal connection if possible.

Independent Practice

Have students work in pairs using a new speed drill. Students will take turns timing each other as they practice the new speed drill.

1. Give all students a new speed drill, charting sheet, timer, file folder, and sticky notes.

2. Tell each student to practice the speed drill three times and chart their growth over the three readings.

3. Instruct students to create a mini speed drill for their partner using the words from their speed drill (or words that contain the skill they were studying): On twenty sticky notes, have students write five words four times, placing them in random order on their open folder.

    ↺ This can be scaffolded up, by having students come up with twenty different words.

    ↺ It can be scaffolded down by giving students sticky notes with words already on them, and all they have to do is mix them up and place them in a random order.

4. Tell students to exchange folders with their partners and each read the words on the folders.

    ↺ As a variation, have students time each other as they read and do repeated readings to see if they can reduce their times.

Stretching Students' Learning

◉ Introduce students to increasingly difficult phonics and orthographic units. For example, explain that "port" is a morpheme that means "to carry," then point out its role in the words *report*, *transport*, *import*, and *export*.

Wear a Word

Activity Overview

For students to be accurate and automatic readers, they must have many exposures to sounds, words, phonics, and orthographic concepts. Wear a Word is a simple, yet fun and effective activity to get students to raise their word consciousness and increase their mastery over words and literacy skills.

In Wear a Word, the teacher and students participate by simply wearing a word badge around their necks. The words that are written on the badges have a connection to concepts taught in the classroom. Attention is drawn to the word badges throughout the day, thereby offering repeated opportunities for students to recognize, hear, and use the word or concept.

Materials

- Index cards to place inside of name badges
- Name badges (the clear, plastic type used at conferences) *or* string for students to use to hang index cards around their necks
- Marker
- Small pictures (*optional*)
- Student whiteboards, dry-erase markers, and erasers
- Chart paper
- Paper

Whole Classroom Instruction

Set the purpose. Say: "In this activity, you will be encountering certain words and concepts throughout the day. The more chances you have to see, hear, and repeat these words and concepts, the more automatic they will become, making you better readers, writers, and spellers."

Choose a set of words that are targeted for vocabulary or a phonics concept, such as short *e* or an orthographic concept like silent *k*. Write one of the words on an index card and insert the card in a name badge. (For more reinforcement with new vocabulary words, you could include on the badge a small picture that represents the word.)

1. Wear your word badge at school.

2. Ask students to read the word in your badge, use the word, explain the word, and write the word as much as possible throughout the day. Whenever a student uses the word in speaking or writing, or notices the targeted word while listening to others, she earns a point.

   - Points can be applied for a variety of things, such as free time, stickers, or a free pass on homework.

Return to the purpose. Say: "Today's activity has helped to expose you to new words throughout the day, which will help you to become better readers, writers, and spellers."

Small Group Work

Write a target skill on index cards and place it inside the name badges. For instance, if the target skill is *igh*, then each badge will have an *igh* pattern word on it, like *night, fright, sight, might*. If the word is a vocabulary word from science, social studies, or a story or novel study, the words would relate to that. If the topic is American history, the words might include *colonists, pioneers, explorers, westward expansion, Native Americans*, etc.

1. Distribute a word badge to each student in the group.

2. Have students read their word to the others in the group.

3. Instruct the students to write all of the words on their whiteboards.

4. Tell students to generate sentences that use the words while you write the sentences on chart paper. Ask students to take turns reading them aloud.

5. Model "coding" the sentences for the target words by putting a circle around any word that is a vocabulary word and a square around any word that is a spelling pattern. For example:

The (Native Americans) helped the first (colonists) [grow] food.

Independent Practice

Have students work in pairs to revisit the text they have been reading and decide together which words follow the pattern (the phonics concept introduced earlier in the day) or are target vocabulary words.

1. Ask students to create (or copy) sentences with the target concepts and copy them onto a piece of paper.

2. Tell students to then code the sentences for the phonics concepts and vocabulary, following the system used in the small group.

Stretching Students' Learning

◎   Wear a Word can be implemented with simple to more complex phonics concepts and sight words, syllable types, or morphemes in which students have already had direct instruction.

Words by Heart

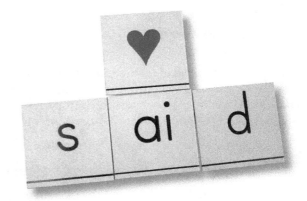

Activity Overview

Students' reading fluency can often be improved by developing automaticity at the word level. The more students know about a word, the better they will be able to read, understand, and spell the word. Good readers and spellers use information about sounds, orthographic patterns, and morphology to help them spell and write words correctly. Words by Heart is an activity that improves fluency by working on the development of automaticity at the word level.

Materials . . . .

- List of spelling words
- Whiteboard (or chart paper), dry-erase markers (including red), and eraser
- Pictures (*optional*)
- Regular red pencils
- Student whiteboards, dry-erase markers (including red), and erasers
- Heart stickers

Whole Classroom Instruction

Set the purpose. Say: "Combining what you are learning about letters and spelling with what you already know about sounds can make you better readers and spellers."

Select a list of spelling words based on a new orthographic pattern, a morpheme that you have taught, or words that are not automatic for the students. You will be "coding" the words one at a time (see examples below) by drawing a heart over the part that needs to be learned by heart. Pictures can also be used to reinforce vocabulary so that the word study is deeper and more connected to vocabulary and comprehension.

1. Write the list of spelling words you have selected on the whiteboard.

2. Say the first word. Tap it out. Ask the students to tap it after you. Discuss the part that "plays fair" and the part that does not play fair. (For more about playing fair, see Picture Perfect Spelling earlier in the Phonics section.)

3. Draw a heart over the part of the word that needs to be learned by heart.

4. Ask students to tap out the other words. Guide them to notice the parts that can be discovered through sound tapping. For example, although the long *i* sound can be heard, its spelling is the part that is tricky in words containing *igh*. Therefore, it is written in red because red means "stop and think." It is the part that cannot be discovered through tapping but needs to be studied and remembered.

5. Discuss vocabulary as it is appropriate, supplementing the spelling words with pictures, gestures, or explanations for students whose language is weak.

Fluency

Examples:

m<u>oo</u>n   b<u>oo</u>m   l<u>oo</u>m

night   Where does the heart go?   n<u>igh</u>t

pickle   Where does the heart go?   pic<u>kle</u>

Return to the purpose. Say: "Practicing heart words helps you to read tricky words more easily."

Small Group Work

1. Display the same spelling list that was used with the whole class and give each student a white board. Then lead students through this activity.

2. Have students read the first word, then tap it out, then write it on their whiteboards, drawing a heart over the tricky part of the word (they can place a sticker instead of drawing a heart).

3. Continue the activity with all the list words, repeating the procedure.

4. When the students have written all the words, ask them to turn to their neighbor and choose a word to use in a sentence, making a connection to their own lives.

5. Using one or two spelling words, model how to continue working on the words before releasing students to perform independent and paired work.

   - Write in pencil a word in the first column.
   - Rewrite the word in the second column, and use a red pencil to draw a heart above the part of the word that does not play fair.
   - Explain that you will close your eyes and visualize the "heart" part of the word. Next, you will visualize the whole word, including the part that needs to be "learned by heart."

6. Finally, fold the paper so that only the third column is showing and rewrite the original word in regular pencil—without the heart this time.

Independent Practice

This portion of the activity combines independent and paired work.

1. Instruct students to continue using the rest of the words on their spelling list, working independently through the same procedure that you modeled earlier.

2. With a partner, have students review all the words together, reading and tapping.

3. Next, have students close their eyes to visualize the words, and then cover the words to try to recall the spelling.

Fluency *Words by Heart*

4. Finally, have them take turns asking each other to give the correct spelling of each word.

Stretching Students' Learning

◉ Words by Heart can be done with multisyllabic words, coding for known morphemes and unfamiliar syllables in the words.

Flyswatter Syllables

Activity Overview

Reading big words demands advanced decoding skills. Moving students from the level of knowing the syllables to recognizing them quickly and automatically can increase their ability to read big words fluently. Reading big words more fluently will have a positive impact on students' ability to comprehend what they read. Flyswatter Syllables emphasizes the development of speed and accuracy in recognizing syllables in words and in isolation.

Materials • • • • • •

- Transparency of a list of syllables
- Overhead projector (or chart paper and tape)
- Flyswatters
- Index cards with syllables and words on them
- Student whiteboards, dry-erase markers, and erasers
- Pictures (*optional*)

Whole Classroom Instruction

Set the purpose. Say: "This activity will give you practice recognizing syllables. Becoming automatic with your ability to recognize syllables will help you to read and understand big words more easily."

1. Divide the class into two teams and have the teams line up on both sides of the room.

2. Display a list of syllables on the overhead projector (or mount on chart paper using tape).

Examples of Syllable Lists

Consonant + *le*:

ble	**cle**	**dle**	**ple**	**gle**

Closed syllable:

con	**fin**	**pan**	**ish**	**dab**

Words with consonant + *le*:

bubble	**barnacle**	**saddle**	**ripple**	**jungle**

3. Call on one student from each team to approach the front of the room, and give them both a flyswatter.

4. Say, for example: "Find the closed syllable." Or, "Which closed syllable says *con*?"
   - The first student to swat the closed syllable with the flyswatter scores one point for her team.

   ⌒ If she can then read the syllable correctly, she will earn an extra point for her team.

5. Have the two students pass their flyswatters to the next students in line and then walk to the end of the line.

6. Repeat this activity until one team is the winner. The pacing should be fast and fun. The goal is to get to automatic recognition.

7. When students are ready, repeat Flyswatter Syllables with multisyllabic words.

Return to the purpose. Say: "You have been practicing recognizing syllables. Becoming automatic with your ability to recognize syllables will help you to read and understand big words more easily."

Small Group Work

1. Place a deck of index cards with the same (or different) syllables that were used for the whole class activity, and another deck with that syllable type embedded within real multisyllabic words, face down in front of the students.

2. Divide the group into two teams, and give one flyswatter to each team.

3. Explain what students will be looking for. For example: "We are looking for magic *e* syllables."

4. Have the teams take turns turning over a card until a magic *e* syllable comes up.

   ⌒ The first person to swat the card with the predetermined syllable type on it gets a point for recognizing it (by sight) quickly.

   ⌒ For another point, the student must sound out the syllable and read it correctly. This point is for decoding the syllable.

   ⌒ Play continues so that there is rapid practice with multiple opportunities for syllable matching.

5. Choose three word cards (for instance, *stable*, *puddle*, and *purple*) and ask students to create sentences using the words and share them with their teammates. Examples: "The horse sleeps in the **stable** every night." "Do not step in the **puddle**!" "**Purple** is the color of my dress."

Independent Practice

Have students work in pairs for more practice with this activity.

1. Give each pair a deck of multisyllabic word cards, a list of what they will be looking for, and two flyswatters.

2. Tell students to check the list to find what they will be looking for, such as, "words with consonant + *le* syllables."

3. Have students divide the deck in half, with each student taking half, and turn over the cards at the same time until they come upon a word that has that syllable type in it, such as *twinkle, table,* or *waffle.* The student who can make a correct match and swat the card the fastest earns a point. Have students play through the deck and keep score themselves.

Stretching Students' Learning

◉ The activity can be done with simple to more complex phonics concepts, sight words, syllable types, or morphemes in which students have already had direct instruction.

Schoolwide Reading

Activity Overview

Students who are fluent readers are more likely to enjoy reading and are therefore motivated to read more words. When they read more words, they learn new words, allowing them to broaden their vocabulary and comprehend what the text means. On the other hand, students who are not fluent readers are less likely to be motivated to read. As a result, they are likely to read fewer words, learn fewer new words, and, because their vocabulary is limited, they are likely to understand less and be less motivated to read more.

Schoolwide Reading emphasizes the development of the motivation to read through the modeling of reading behaviors by all school personnel, family members, and students. It does not involve sustained silent reading during the instructional reading block. Rather, it is meant to bring models of reading through activities like reading together in small groups, partner reading, and read-alouds during dedicated reading time outside of the instructional reading block.

Materials • • • • • •

- Camera
- Books
- Supplies for making and displaying posters

Schoolwide Activity

Set the purpose. Say: "When you spend time reading, you can become better readers. When you spend time listening and being read to, it will build your ability to listen and understand. During Schoolwide Reading, you will have the opportunity to read and be read to."

Hold an assembly in which the principal will introduce Schoolwide Reading. Have the principal launch a reading project for which she will start every assembly by either reading a story or telling part of a progressive story for a few minutes each week.

Schoolwide Reading involves everyone in a school dedicating some time each day (or several days out of the week) to read with children. Before you begin the activity, take pictures of school personnel, family members, and students reading, such as:

- Kitchen staff reading cookbooks
- Athletic staff reading sports biographies
- Music teacher reading books about music or composers
- Teachers reading their favorite books
- Teachers reading books to groups of students
- Parents reading with children

- Grandparents reading with children

- Older students reading with younger students

- Older students reading their favorite books in comfortable places

- Office staff and principal reading books and reading with children

Food service workers reading cookbooks.

Additionally, photograph people in the school who can read a foreign language (such as parents of English language learners) reading books in their native languages. Make posters of your pictures and put them up all around school.

Talking Classroom

- Dedicate time each day for reading together in groups, pairs, or read-alouds.

- Allow some time after reading for oral language practice with discussion about the story, book, etc.

- Have meetings at school for parents in which you encourage them to read aloud to their children.

- Train parents in strategies that can help them make the most of their reading time at home with their children.

- Give parents the opportunity for a free schoolwide book fair. Using school funds, buy new books, go to used book sales and collect children's books, or collect donated used children's books. Let parents "shop" for books that they can own and take home and read to their children. Giving parents the opportunity to self-select books for their homes is empowering and adds to their investment and the likelihood that they will follow through and read to their children.

- Use school funds to find as many other native language children's books as you can. Have books available for parents at your free book fair in their native language. Be sure to order children's books in Spanish if there is a population of Spanish-speaking parents at your school. Books in Vietnamese, Russian, and other languages are available on the Internet and in some bookstores.

- Involve older siblings when parents do not know how to read or are working and are not available to read to children.

- Consider a literacy project at your school for teaching parents to read.

Vocabulary Activities

31. Making Words My Own

32. How Well Do I Know It?

33. Flyswatter Morphemes

34. Bringing Words to Scale

35. Word Webs

36. A Special Word

37. Sports Card Words

38. Word Train

39. Branching Out

40. Schoolwide Vocabulary

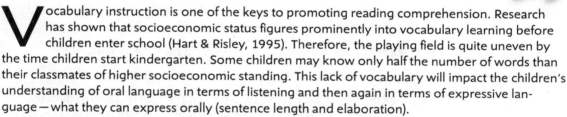

Vocabulary instruction is one of the keys to promoting reading comprehension. Research has shown that socioeconomic status figures prominently into vocabulary learning before children enter school (Hart & Risley, 1995). Therefore, the playing field is quite uneven by the time children start kindergarten. Some children may know only half the number of words than their classmates of higher socioeconomic standing. This lack of vocabulary will impact the children's understanding of oral language in terms of listening and then again in terms of expressive language—what they can express orally (sentence length and elaboration).

Shining a light on word-learning activities is a great use of time, not just during students' early school years but throughout their entire academic career. In kindergarten through third grade, students learn more words by listening—but then the balance shifts and they learn more new words from reading them. If students are not fluent readers who enjoy reading, they are less likely to read and thus more likely to learn fewer words than their counterparts who are fluent readers. This, in turn, will impact their ability to comprehend text because their vocabulary is limited.

There are different levels of word learning. A word can be unknown (students have never heard the word), known (students know the word but do not use it in their speaking and writing vocabulary), or the word can be "owned." When a word is owned, it can be defined and understood at an automatic level. It is well attached to neural networks of other words, ideas, and concepts, and therefore the brain can easily recall and retrieve the word. Two vocabulary strategies presented in this book involve chunking and linking words and information. These activities encourage students to make connections with prior learning and experience and sort and categorize words that go together.

The vocabulary activities in this section are designed to enhance students' word consciousness. An effective way to motivate word consciousness is to positively reinforce students when they listen for a word in speech, watch for a word in print, and use the word correctly in their speaking and writing. Reinforcement can take the form of points that can be applied toward rewards, such as time with the teacher, a pass on homework, or computer privileges. Students need to learn more words than their teachers can individually teach. Word consciousness gets students involved in expanding their own word learning and develops responsibility for vocabulary development.

The Four Processing Systems Connection

For students to be able to read vocabulary words, they first must be able to decode them. Students need to know the sound/symbol connection, which engages both the phonological and orthographic processors. At the same time, students must know the meaning of the words and be able to use the words in a sentence, which engages the meaning and context processors. This section's activities are designed to involve all four processing systems to maximize vocabulary development.

The LETRS Connection

◎ *Language Essentials for Teachers of Reading and Spelling* (LETRS), Module 4—*The Mighty Word*.

◎ *Language Essentials for Teachers of Reading and Spelling* (LETRS), Module 11—*Comprehension Through Writing*.

The Assessment Connection

◎ *DIBELS: Dynamic Indicators of Basic Early Literacy Skills.* Word Use Fluency.

◎ *DIBELS: Dynamic Indicators of Basic Early Literacy Skills.* Oral Reading Fluency: Assesses level of automaticity with hearing and segmenting sounds within spoken words.

The ELL Connection

Many of the activities in this section will be effective with ELLs without any alteration. However, a few small changes can have a great impact on the achievement and skill development for these students. The following are a few ideas to try that may enhance the effectiveness of the vocabulary activities:

◎ These activities can be easily adapted to students learning in their native language.

◎ Scaffold word learning with pictures, objects, and gestures for deeper comprehension.

◎ Activities that emphasize the morphological structure of English can be used to directly teach the similarities between the student's first language and English (shared morphemes).

◎ Drawing illustrations for words, phrases, sentences, and longer text can help teach students to create mental images as they listen, read, and write.

◎ There are so many words for ELLs to acquire. Learning words in networks of words accelerates word learning and ties new learning to previous learning. Making these connections can deepen ownership of new words in the student's new language.

◎ Many of the activities can be done with a combination of primary and secondary language words. For example, if the target word in a Word Web or Branching Out activity is *weather*, you could write the word in English and in Spanish (*weather, el tiempo*) and invite students to complete the web using words from either language. This modification will help students link new words to old words and enhance the transition to a new language.

◎ You can use many of the activities to stimulate meta-linguistic thinking by asking students to compare and contrast words in their native language to words in English.

◎ Use new words in sentences to model and help students comprehend new vocabulary to enhance word learning. Illustrating and using gestures also helps students gain a deeper understanding of new words.

◎ Group and partner work provides modeling for oral language that is helpful to ELLs. In addition, the small group and partner settings offer environments that encourage more risk taking in the area of oral language.

Dig In to Learn More

Beck, I.L., McKeown, M.G., & Kucan, L. (2002). *Bringing words to life: Robust vocabulary instruction*. New York; Guilford Press.

Ebbers, Susan M. (2004). *Vocabulary through morphemes*. Longmont, CO: Sopris West Educational Services.

Moats, L. C. (2005). *Language essentials for teachers of reading and spelling (LETRS), Module 4—The Mighty Word*. Longmont, CO: Sopris West Educational Services.

Vocabulary Activities

Making Words My Own

Activity Overview

Students need to learn many new words on an ongoing basis to develop good comprehension skills. Developing word consciousness is an important goal of vocabulary instruction. When students have word consciousness, they are aware of words in their environment and enjoy engaging in word learning.

Making personal connections to words is one strategy that deepens word learning. While understanding the meaning of a word is important, it takes more than just knowing a definition to truly "own" a word. Numerous meaningful exposures to the word include opportunities to make connections between the word's meaning and students' lives. Making Words My Own emphasizes word learning that connects the meaning with a personal connection, a picture, and a plan for remembering the word in an effort to increase retention and retrieval of the words studied.

Materials

- Whiteboard (or chart paper), dry-erase marker, and eraser
- Colored pencils (or crayons)
- Lists of target vocabulary words
- Index cards for making word study cards

Whole Classroom Instruction

Set the purpose. Say: "In this activity, you are going to learn a lot about words—beyond just their definition. As you begin to make personal connections to the words, you will find it easier to remember and use the words. Knowing more words will make you better at listening, speaking, reading, and writing."

1. Using a whiteboard, draw two horizontal rectangles and divide each by drawing a vertical line down the middle (see the illustration on the following page). These boxes represent the word study cards students will be creating from index cards. In the left box, write the target word.

2. Label the four boxes as follows:
   - **What Is It?** (Define it.)
   - **Label the Bucket: Words That Connect** (The bucket refers to the main idea, the overarching category that the word represents.)
   - **Picture** (Draw a picture and use the word in a sentence.)
   - **My Plan to Remember** (How will I connect?)

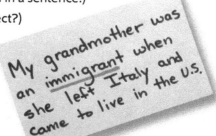

Immigrant

Front of card:

What Is It?	Label the Bucket: Words That Connect

Back of card:

Picture	My Plan to Remember

3. Generate ideas from the class for filling in the boxes and write them on the whiteboard.

Immigrant

Front of card:

What Is It?	Label the Bucket: Words That Connect
Word: immigrant An **immigrant** is a person who leaves her home country to live in a new country.	airplane, boats, new language, trains, new school, work, different culture, safety, money

Back of card:

Picture	My Plan to Remember
Many people in America are **immigrants** who have come from many different countries.	1. I will remember because my family and my friend Rosa's family are immigrants from Mexico. 2. We also have a boy in our class who is an immigrant from Africa. 3. I will think that the first letter is "I" and I am an immigrant.

4. These cards are invaluable for studying vocabulary. Students who create these cards will be able to study the words later.

↺ Students should be able to look at the word, the definition, and words related to the original word and recall the picture they have made to associate with the word as well as the connection they made to help themselves recall the word.

↺ Students should also be able to look at the picture and their plan for recalling the word (their connection with the word) and remember the word.

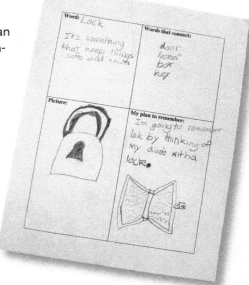

Return to the purpose. Say: "Making connections with words can deepen your understanding of them and will help you to remember and use the words. When you know more words, you can become better readers, writers, speakers and listeners."

Small Group Work

1. Give students an index card and colored pencils.

2. Preteach target vocabulary words that come from reading or units of study.

3. Tell students to choose one of the words and fill in their card following the teacher's model during whole class instruction.

4. Guide as needed, with immediate responsive feedback as students complete their word study card.

5. Have students show their work to the group, read their notes on the word, share their picture, and discuss how they plan to remember the word.

Independent Practice

Have students work with a partner for this portion of the activity.

1. Give each student two index cards a list of target vocabulary words, sheet protectors, and colored pencils.

2. Have students independently complete the two word study cards and place them in sheet protectors.

3. Tell students to discuss their two new cards with each other.

4. Ask them to then test each other on all three words they have written about (one they wrote about in the small group and two they wrote about independently), starting with the word and going to the definition, the characteristics, and then describing their picture and their plan for remembering the word.

5. For a second time, have the partners show their picture, then go from the picture to the word and definition, ending again with their plan for remembering the word.

6. If the partners have chosen different words, challenge them to learn each other's words, not just their own.

Stretching Students' Learning

◉ Increase the number of words students study.

◉ For students with better language skills, increase the complexity of words, or use a root as a basis for the study of whole networks of words (see Branching Out, later in this section).

How Well Do I Know It?

large

enormity

Activity Overview

How well students know a word makes a difference in their ability to read it fluently, retrieve it for speaking, understand it when listening, and use it in writing. The three levels of word knowledge are:

- ◎ **Unknown—Students have never heard the word.** They have never encountered the word before in reading or listening.

- ◎ **Known—Students know the word.** They have heard the word before. They understand it in context but don't know it well enough to use it themselves in speaking or writing.

- ◎ **Own—Students "own" the word.** They know it well enough to define it and use it in their speaking and writing.

Materials • • • • • • •

- ◎ Index cards
- ◎ Marker
- ◎ Magnetic or sticky tape
- ◎ Whiteboard, dry-erase markers, and eraser
- ◎ Sticky notes
- ◎ Pictures with magnetic or sticky tape on back (*optional*)
- ◎ File folders

This activity will help you to informally assess and track students' level of word knowledge and monitor progress toward word mastery. It allows you to observe the number of meaningful repetitions it may take for different students to move from not knowing a word to mastering and owning that word. How Well Do I Know It? should be part of an overall effort to enhance word consciousness by positively reinforcing students' efforts to listen for a word in speech, watch for a word in print, and use the word correctly in their speaking and writing.

Whole Classroom Instruction

Set the purpose. Say: "You can know words in different ways. Sometimes you have never heard a word and you know nothing about it. Other times you have heard a word but aren't quite sure what it means. Then there are those words that you "own"! That means you know them so well that you use them when you speak and write. Today you are going to explore how well you know words. All year you will be learning fun ways to get to own as many words as you can."

Unknown	Known	Own

Before the activity, take three index cards and write the words *Unknown, Known,* and *Own.* Add magnetic or sticky tape to the back of the cards and place the cards as column headings on the whiteboard. Write the words to be taught on separate sticky notes (for example, *responsibility, discover,* etc.). The new words may be from a story that will be read or from a social studies, math, or science unit to be studied.

Students make decisions about how well they know words.

1. Discuss each new vocabulary word you've selected and decide if the class as a whole knows it, owns it, or if it is completely unknown. You may have different levels of word knowledge for each word. Decide in which column to place the sticky note.

   ☺ If some of your more advanced students know a word that is unknown to others, you may make a goal for them that they use it in their speaking and writing in class.

   ☺ Optionally, add a picture to each column to help students form a mental image as a way of scaffolding, if necessary. This additional strategy can deepen word learning and word consciousness.

2. Graphing word learning: Create a living word wall, combining it with graph reading. Make a display with three columns. As new words are introduced, place them under Unknown. As students demonstrate that they know the words, move the words to the Known column. The students can watch the bars of words they own grow bigger and see growth in their word knowledge as words move from Unknown to Known to Own.

Return to the purpose. Say: "You've been discovering how well you know words. When you own words, that means you know them so well that you can use them when you speak and write. All year you will be learning fun ways to get to own as many words as you can."

Small Group Work

This activity can give students meaningful repetition of the target words in a small group setting. Give each student a folder and sticky notes.

1. Draw three columns on a whiteboard and label the columns "Unknown," "Known," and "Own."

2. Have students create a vocabulary folder for the vocabulary for the week or unit of study in which they will keep a chart of words and their level of word knowledge.

3. Write the target vocabulary words on small sticky notes. The sticky notes can be moved from Unknown to Known and finally Own. When the sticky notes reach the Own column, students can record the words in their notebooks.

4. Have students participate in activities that use the target words. For instance, students can use a word by creating a definition of the word as a group, such as: "**Responsibility** is when a person is given a special job to do, like feeding a dog or taking care of a younger brother or sister."

Vocabulary

5. Ask students to turn to a neighbor and use the word in a sentence. Examples: "I have the **responsibility** of clearing my dishes from the table after dinner each night." "A detective can **discover** who committed a crime."

Independent Practice

For this portion of the activity, have students work with a partner to increase their mastery of using target vocabulary words.

1. Distribute file folders students created during small group work.

2. Next, ask students to orally rehearse a sentence for each word with their partner and then write their sentences on a separate piece of paper.

   ↻ This will be at least the third time during the day that students encounter and use a target word in a meaningful way.

   ↻ This kind of repetition and reinforcement of words not only develops word ownership and an expansion of vocabulary, but it helps students to become word-conscious readers, listeners, speakers, and writers.

Stretching Students' Learning

   ⟳ Students can create folders with words they encounter in reading that they might know but aren't using in their speaking and writing. Words can be taken from research projects, science, social studies, or math.

Flyswatter Morphemes

Activity Overview

Reading big words demands advanced decoding skills. Because English is a morpho-phonological language, students are better equipped to read big words when they have had systematic instruction in both the syllable types and morphemes of the language. Flyswatter Morphemes is an activity that emphasizes the development of speed and accuracy with morpheme recognition in words and in isolation. Moving students from knowing the morphemes to recognizing them quickly and automatically can increase their ability to read big words fluently. Morphemes can help reveal the meanings of new words. Increasing vocabulary plus improving fluency can have a powerful impact on reading comprehension.

Materials • • • • • • •

- Transparency of morpheme list
- Overhead projector (or chart paper and tape)
- Flyswatters
- Index cards with morphemes on them; index cards with multisyllabic words on them containing the same morphemes
- Pictures (*optional*)

Whole Classroom Instruction

Set the purpose. Say: "This activity will give you practice recognizing morphemes quickly and accurately. Becoming automatic with your ability to recognize morphemes will help you to read and understand big words more easily."

1. Divide the class into two teams and have the teams line up on both sides of the room.

2. Put a list of morphemes that have been previously taught on the overhead projector. It might look something like the following:

   | mis- | re- | dis- | un- | pre- | sub- |
   | anti- | non- | uni- | trans- | bi- | tri- |

3. Call on one student from each team to approach the front of the room and give both students a flyswatter.

4. Say, for example: "Find the prefix that means 'do again.'"
   - The first student to swat the prefix *re-* with the flyswatter scores one point for his team.
   - If he can then read the syllable correctly, he will get an extra point for his team.
   - The two students pass their flyswatters to the next students in line and then walk to the end of the line.

5. Repeat this activity for a specified time. At the end of that time, the team with the most points wins. The pacing should be fast and fun. The goal is to get to automatic recognition.

6. When students are ready, repeat this activity with multisyllabic words.

Return to the purpose. Say: "You have been practicing recognizing morphemes. Becoming automatic in recognizing morphemes will help you read and understand big words more easily."

Small Group Work

1. Place a deck of index cards with the same (or different) morphemes (prefixes, suffixes, or roots) that were used in the whole class activity, and another deck with those morphemes embedded within real multisyllabic words, face down in front of the students.

Students work on fluency with morphemes.

2. Divide the small group into two teams and give each team a flyswatter.

3. Explain what the students will be looking for. For example: "You will be looking for prefixes."

4. Have the teams take turns turning over a card until the predetermined morpheme type (in this case prefixes) comes up.
    ☙ The first person to swat the card with the prefix on it gets a point.
    ☙ For another point, the student must sound out and read the morpheme correctly (decoding).

5. Have students continue to play so that there is rapid practice with multiple opportunities for morpheme matching.

Talking Classroom

6. Choose three morpheme cards (for instance, *mis-*, *re-*, and *de-*) and ask the students to create sentences using the morphemes and share them with their team. For example: "He made one **mistake** on his spelling test." "I asked her to **redo** the chart." "If you crush your hand, you might **deform** it."

Independent Practice

Have students work in pairs for more practice.

1. Give each pair a deck of multisyllabic words, a list of what they will be looking for, and a flyswatter.

2. Tell students to check the list to find what they will be looking for, such as, "words with prefixes that mean 'not.'"

3. Have students continue to turn over the cards until they come upon a word that has that target morpheme in it, like *unkind* or *dislike*. The student who can make a correct match and swat the card the fastest earns a point.

4. Ask students to write down the word in their notebooks under a new heading called "Morpheme Speed Words."

Stretching Students' Learning

◎ Increase the difficulty of the level of roots, prefixes, and suffixes.

◎ Use academic words as a source for morphemes (e.g., *microscope*, *microscopic*, *stethoscope*).

Bringing Words to Scale

Activity Overview

Students' ability to express themselves is enhanced when they have knowledge of words that are related. Sometimes we think of the connection between words as related to the same topic or concept, such as words about cooking or words with the prefix *pre-*. In Bringing Words to Scale, students will think about and use words that are related by their degree of similarity and difference. Starting with a pair of opposites, such as *hot* and *cold*, students can fill in words that are related to the antonyms in terms of meaning. For instance, *hot* and *cold* can involve a scale: **hot**—*warm*—*cool*—**cold.** Students can go beyond the opposites to more descriptive words: **scorching**—*scalding*—*sizzling*—*boiling*—*steaming*—**hot**—*tepid*—*warm*—*lukewarm*—*cool*—*chilly*—**cold**—*freezing*—**frigid.**

This activity requires that students think about words in relationship to each other and that they compare their thinking about the words to that of their classmates. This meta-cognitive thinking about language enhances word learning, retention, and retrieval.

Materials

- Marker and card stock
- Plastic hand clappers* (*optional*)
- Student whiteboards, dry-erasers markers, and erasers
- Word Line Worksheet (see Appendix A)
- Index cards
- Rope and clothespins
- Pictures (*optional*)
- Plastic sheet protectors
- Sticky notes
- File folders

* Available in the optional Classroom Manipulatives Kit

Whole Classroom Instruction

Set the purpose. Say: "Learning new describing words can help you to express yourself better in speaking and writing. In this activity, you will be thinking of words that are similar to each other and words that are different. When you know and understand a lot of words, you will be able to describe things more precisely."

Prior to the activity, prepare a set of word cards using a marker and card stock. Write antonyms and words that fit somewhere in between the opposite words. Write one word per card.

1. Distribute blank pieces of card stock and hand clappers to everyone, if available.

2. Distribute cards upon which you have written words to some students.

3. Ask students who have the cards with the words on them to come up to the front of the room.

4. Meanwhile, introduce a pair of opposite words, and ask students at their desks to think about words that fit in between the opposites and to write some of their ideas on their whiteboards.

5. Ask students at the front to arrange themselves, according to their cards, in an order that makes sense going from one opposite to the other. Have them line up with their cards in front of them, facing the class.

hot	lukewarm	cool	cold

6. Tell students who are seated that if they know a word that can be added to the line, they should write it on their blank card and get in line where they think they belong.

7. Have students at their desks clap their clappers (or their hands) if they agree with the order.

8. Explain that students who think the order could be rearranged should raise their hand and make their suggestions about the order of the words.

Return to the purpose. Say: "You have been thinking about words that are similar and different. When you know and understand a lot of words that describe things, you will become better readers, writers, and speakers."

Small Group Work

1. Give students a pair of antonyms to work with and a Word Line Worksheet.

2. As a group, decide on some words that fit in between the antonyms you are discussing, for example, *big* and *small*, *peace* and *war*, *light* and *heavy*. Using index cards, write down all the words the students suggest.

Students work together to sort words.

3. Hang a rope from the board or lay it out on the reading table. Attach the index cards in an order that makes sense to the "word line" using clothespins.

   ↻ Provide pictures to help those students who might need this scaffolding strategy. Pictures can help students deepen word learning and word consciousness. Pictures can also be hung on the word line.

4. Discuss with the group the order of the words. Ask students to comment on whether they agree or not with the order. Change the order if students can provide convincing reasons for doing so.

5. Instruct students to copy onto their Word Line Worksheet the words from the word line that are in the correct order and have been "brought to scale."

6. Next, have students choose one of the words and use it in a sentence under the word line on their worksheets. When finished, ask them to put their worksheet in a plastic sheet protector and place it in their notebook.

7. Hang the word line up somewhere in the classroom.

Independent Practice

In this portion of the activity, partners work together to sort word cards and discuss why they are choosing a particular order for the words.

1. Distribute word cards, sticky notes, file folders, and a Word Line Worksheet to everyone.

2. Tell students to copy the words from the cards onto the sticky notes and to arrange the notes in a mixed-up order on the top half of their folder, creating a sorting activity for another student.

3. During this activity or later, have another student take the folder and decide which of the words on the sticky notes represent opposites and place the others in between them.

4. Have students copy the words they have been working with onto their Word Line Worksheet and then place the worksheet in their notebook.

5. Ask students to orally rehearse a good sentence that uses one or two of their favorite words of the words they have sorted. Tell them to write that sentence at the bottom of their Word Line Worksheet before placing it in their notebook.

Stretching Students' Learning

◎ Relate the words that are used in this activity to characters, settings, and themes being studied to enhance comprehension and oral and written expression.

Word Webs

Activity Overview

Word webs are graphic organizers designed to help students form concepts about words in relationship to other words they might know. A word web shows graphically that words are associated. This activity emphasizes learning words in relationship to one another. Using words that are related facilitates vocabulary development and word consciousness.

Word webs can be part of an overall effort to enhance word consciousness by giving positive reinforcement to students for their willingness and ability to listen for words in speech, watch for words in print, and use words themselves in speaking and writing.

Materials

- Index cards and colored pencils or markers
- Magnetic tape (*optional*)
- Whiteboard (or chart paper), dry-erase marker, and eraser
- Pictures
- Word Web Worksheet (see Appendix A)
- Stapler
- Pieces of yarn
- Plastic sheet protectors
- Partially completed Word Web Worksheet (*optional*)

Whole Classroom Instruction

Set the purpose. Say: "This activity will help you learn words in relation to other words. Learning words that are related makes them easier to understand, remember, and use."

Prior to the activity, determine the target words that you will introduce. The words may be from a story that will be read or from a unit of study. On index cards, write the main target word, such as *weather,* and other related target words, such as *temperature, rain,* and *snow.* Optionally, apply magnetic tape to the back of each card so that the cards can be mounted on a whiteboard.

1. Introduce the target words to the class and explain each word's meaning.

2. Draw a web on the whiteboard, beginning with a simple circle. (Or arrange cards with magnetic tape on the whiteboard.)

3. Write the main target word in the middle of the circle (or on top of the web). Place a picture (that has magnetic tape on the back) beneath the word to help students create a mental image. Add one or two words to the web on the board to model for students.

4. Distribute the preprinted index cards to several students. Distribute some blank cards as well. (Not all students will have a card.)

5. **Creating a Living Word Web**: Ask that the student who has the card with the main target word (*weather*) on it to move to the front of the room (or somewhere in the room with adequate space for a group of students).

6. One by one, have students with preprinted cards read their cards aloud and then move to the front of the room, positioning themselves around the student holding the main idea word.

7. Have students at the front read their words aloud again, so that the entire web is reviewed.

8. Discuss the web with the class.
   - Students with blank cards may write a word that fits and come up and join the web. For example, a student might write *cloudy* on a card and then join the Living Word Web for the word *weather*.

9. While students remain in the web formation, write the web on the board.

10. Have students return to their seats. Distribute copies of the Word Web Worksheet and instruct everyone to copy the web onto it.
    - If students can think of more words than they have spaces for, they can add in their own circles as they copy the web.

11. Consider displaying a copy of the completed word web up on the wall as part of a vocabulary living word wall.

Return to the purpose. Say: "You have been learning words in relation to other words. When you learn words in relation to other words, they become easier to understand, remember, and use."

Small Group Work

1. Distribute two blank index cards to each student.

2. Place a new target word card in the middle of the table.

3. Discuss the target word and have the group generate words together that are related to the target word. Make a list of all the students' words that fit the web concept on a whiteboard or on chart paper.

4. Using the target word in the middle of the table, have students work together to create a web using their blank index cards—each student will add one word to the web.
   - Guide students to use the correct spelling of the words by consulting the list you created on the whiteboard.

5. Next, tell students to draw a quick sketch (on their remaining index card) to illustrate their word and place it next to the word card.

6. Use a stapler to attach the new words to the target word and then to attach the picture cards to the word cards. This can be used as a quick reinforcement and can be hung on a wall or kept in a file for quick review in the future.

Independent Practice

With a partner, students will work on the floor or at tables and create original word webs.

1. Distribute index cards and pieces of yarn to everyone.

2. Suggest that students choose a main target word that is related to a unit of study, the target vocabulary words introduced earlier, or a theme in which they have a special interest. Explain that they will make a word web with their partner using yarn to connect their cards. Have them use a stapler to attach the yarn and form a web similar to the webs completed earlier.

    ᴄ For students who need more structure, you can give them a prepared set of cards and a partially completed Word Web Worksheet.

3. Students prepare one web together, taking turns adding an index card.

4. Tell students to copy their web in a section of their notebook labeled "Vocabulary Word Webs." Place webs in a plastic sheet protector.

5. If time allows, have each set of students share their web work with the larger group, giving their reasons for creating the web in the way they chose.

Stretching Students' Learning

◉ Increase the number of words students study.

◉ For students with better language skills, increase the complexity of target words, or use a root as a basis for the study of whole networks of words (see Branching Out later in the Vocabulary section). For example, you can use *spect* as the target and build the web using the words *spectacle*, *spectator*, *introspective*, *respect*, and *spectrum*.

A Special Word

I closed the latch on the box to keep it shut.

latch

Activity Overview

Context is critical for learning new words. We can look up words in the dictionary and still not know their meaning because relevant context is missing. When we teach words in the classroom, we need to make the context clear and understandable.

A Special Word develops and reinforces the ability to think about words and their meaning by encouraging students to examine the context in which the words are used. Learning words in isolation is of limited value—it is important for students to be able to use the words correctly. This activity gives students practice choosing a new, "special" word and writing a sentence using the word that would help other readers understand what the word means.

A Special Word emphasizes 100 percent engagement of the class in word learning. This activity should be part of an overall effort to enhance word consciousness by positively reinforcing students' efforts when they listen for a word in speech, watch for a word in print, and use the word correctly in their speaking and writing.

Materials . . . .

- ⟲ Index cards
- ⟲ Whiteboard, dry-erase marker, and eraser
- ⟲ Colored pencils or markers
- ⟲ Chart paper

Whole Classroom Instruction

Set the purpose. Say: "You will be teaching others new words in this activity by using the words in good sentences and sharing those sentences with each other. The meaning of the new words should be so clear from your sentences that the person reading them will be able to make a mental picture of the words."

1. Model this activity first by thinking of a special word (one that the class may not be familiar with), such as *philanthropic*.
   - ℃ Write the word on the board and ask students to think about the meaning of the word.
   - ℃ Use the word in a sentence: "I am **philanthropic** when I share my time, money, or things to help others who have less than I do." The sentence should model that a good sentence can teach the meaning of a word by making the context clear and directly related to the word. Encourage students to form a picture in their mind from reading the sentence.

2. Pass out one index card to sets of partners in the class. Tell students to clear their desks so that the only thing on top is the card.

3. Ask each pair to think of a "special" word that they know because of a personal interest or an activity they have done, or an interesting word they have heard or read.

- If students have difficulty coming up with a word, guide them with a word that is within their language ability level.

4. Tell the pair to write their word on one side of their index card and then turn the card over and write the word in a sentence. Remind them to make sure the sentence will help readers form a mental picture of what the word means. When they are finished, ask them to turn the card back over to have only the word showing.

5. Have partners move around the room together and read as many other partner's cards as time will allow.

  - Tell students to see if they know the word before turning over the card. If they think they know the word, they should discuss it with their partner.

  - If they don't know the word, they can turn the card over to try to figure out what the word means from the sentence. Partners should help each other figure out the word if it is still unclear.

6. When students have had a chance to read most of their classmates' sentences, ask them to return to their seats and discuss with you some of the words and sentences they have been reading and which words they liked learning the best.

7. Add students' favorite words to a class word wall.

Return to the purpose. Say: "You have been sharing and learning new words. Writing sentences that explain words clearly helps readers make pictures in their mind when they read your words. Pictures can help us remember words better."

Small Group Work

A Special Word can work well as a small group activity, using target words that are being emphasized in classroom instruction.

1. Distribute index cards and pencils or markers.

2. Write the target words on a whiteboard.

3. Working as a small group, have students select one of the target words, such as *responsibility,* and take turns using it in context.

4. Write the sentences that students generate on chart paper. For instance: "In my family I have the **responsibility** of feeding our puppy."

5. On the other side of the card, have students write the word and a quick sketch to go with the sentence they made up. (They do not have to write the sentence because you will do that for the group; however, encourage those students who are capable to write the sentence below their sketch.)

Independent Practice

For more practice, students can work with a partner using a set of target vocabulary words. Write the words on index cards prior to the activity.

Vocabulary A Special Word

1. Give students a set of 3–5 index cards with the target words on them.

2. Ask partners to create a sentence on the back of each card using the words in context. Partners can take turns writing the sentences.

3. Tell students to choose any three of the sentences and copy them into their notebook. If they think their partner's sentence is more descriptive than their own, they may use their partner's sentence instead.

Stretching Students' Learning

- This is an activity that gets all students engaged in stretching the level of their vocabulary knowledge.

- Students can act out target vocabulary words.

Sports Card Words

Activity Overview

Graphic organizers and concept webs help students learn information by organizing concepts, words, and information. Sports cards are wonderful examples of how a lot of information can be arranged and codified in a systematic manner. They have a picture (which provides a mental image) and a grid of details that support the main topic. Everything is structured in an organized manner.

Sports Card Words is an activity that can be used before, during, and after a reading activity. It will help students organize their word knowledge in terms of what they already know and will help them add what they have learned to their original ideas about the words. The model of sports cards can be used for individual words or a theme, with different words being networked around that theme.

Materials
- Chart paper and marker
- Baseball Card Worksheet (see Appendix A)
- Sports or baseball cards

Whole Classroom Instruction

Set the purpose. Say: "In this activity, you will be organizing information and combining it with a picture. This method of organizing makes learning fun and easy and will help you understand and use information better in your reading and writing."

1. On a piece of chart paper draw a blank baseball card template similar to the worksheet students will be using.

2. Choose a word or theme that will be the target for instruction and write it at the top of the card—for example, *colonists*.

3. Draw a quick sketch in the picture section of the card that illustrates the vocabulary word or theme—for example, a picture of a colonist.

4. Add a definition of the word or a brief description of the theme. For example, "**Colonists** were people who came from Europe to settle in the New World."

5. Draw a second box that will represent the back of the sports card template.

6. Fill out additional information about the word—connect it to other words (e.g., *settlers, freedom, communities*), use it in a sentence with one of the other words (e.g., "The **colonists** lived in small communities."), add a synonym, add an antonym, provide multiple meanings, etc.

Return to the purpose. Say: "Organizing information and combining it with a picture makes learning fun and easy. When you organize information, it can improve your reading and writing."

Small Group Work

1. Place a selection of sports or baseball cards on the table for the group to explore.

2. Using a blank Baseball Card Worksheet, create a group baseball card based on a word or topic chosen by the group.

   ↺ Draw a quick picture and fill out the back of the card while students supply additional information about the word or topic.

3. Have students turn to a neighbor and restate the word or topic and use the details from the back of the card to help describe the word or topic.

Independent Practice

Have students work with a partner for additional practice with this activity.

1. Give each student a blank Baseball Card Worksheet.

2. Ask partners to choose a topic to work on. If they can't agree, they may each select their own topic of interest. It can be a topic studied in class, a story read together or independently, or a topic of personal interest to them.

3. Instruct each partner to draw his own picture and then work cooperatively with his partner to fill in the back of their cards, sharing ideas and information.

4. Display the finished cards on a sports card word wall titled "Words: Most Valuable Players—MVP Words We Know." Hang the cards from a string so that both sides can be visible.

Stretching Students' Learning

   ◉ Discuss the target words in relation to characters, settings, and themes being studied to enhance comprehension and oral and written expression.

thermometer

a tool for measuring temperature (hot and cold)

My mother uses a thermometer when I am sick.

Word Train

Activity Overview

Vocabulary instruction is most effective when it involves word study that goes beyond the definition of the word alone. Word Train gives students opportunities to learn a lot about a target word: the sounds, syllables, morphemes, antonyms, synonyms, and other words that are related to the target word. The more students know about a word, the more likely they will be to recall its meaning for listening and reading, and retrieve the word for speaking and writing.

Materials • • • • • • •

- Index cards with magnetic tape on the back (or large sticky notes) (*optional*)
- Marker (*optional*)
- Pieces of paper (*optional*)
- Index cards for students
- Pencils, colored pencils, markers, and/or crayons
- Word Train Worksheet (see Appendix A)

Whole Classroom Instruction

Set the purpose. Say: "The more you know about words, the easier it will be for you to remember and use them as you speak, listen, read, and write. This activity will give you practice in organizing the information you know about words to help you learn the words much better."

Word Train is appropriate for all grade levels—the only difference would be the level of word study, the number of related words the students might come up with, and details about the word, including more information about morphemes.

1. Model building a word train on the front board using a story that all the students have been reading or listening to or a theme they have been studying in any content area. Draw seven boxes (see the following instructions) and fill them in to represent the cars of the train, or use index cards with magnetic tape on the back. (Modeling could also be done on the floor using pieces of paper to build the train with the students seated in a circle on the floor.)

   Car #1. Write the study word, for instance, *thermometer*.

   Car #2. Write a simple definition, such as, "A tool for measuring temperature—hot and cold."

   Car #3. Draw a picture of a thermometer.

   Car #4. Ask students to provide various pieces of information about the word. Two examples include the number of syllables (four) and the origin of the word (Greek).

   Car #5. Ask for suggestions and write a few related words, such as *weather* and *sick*.

   Car #6. Write a sentence using the word: "My mother uses a **thermometer** when I am sick."

Car #7. Create a plan, or a link, to help remember the word: "I will remember that we have a **thermometer** outside the window of our classroom." (At a higher level, a student might say, "***Therm*** is a morpheme that relates to heat, and we have a thermos in my family that my Dad takes to work to keep his coffee hot.")

Return to the purpose. Say: "Organizing what you know about words and linking that to other words and information you already know helps you to understand more, make deeper connections, and be able to share what you have learned more easily. This activity will give you practice in organizing what you know about words to help you learn the words better."

Small Group Work

Students will work as a group on a new target vocabulary word to create a word train following the model that was made during the whole class instruction.

1. Distribute seven index cards to each student. Provide pencils, colored pencils, markers, and/or crayons, as needed. (You can also use the Word Train Worksheet for this activity.)

2. Guide students to use the same activity that was modeled earlier, creating seven train cars and adding information for each car: (1) the word; (2) the definition; (3) a picture of the word; (4) a sentence using the word; (5) information about the word (number of syllables, origin, morphemes, etc.); (6) related words; and (7) a link—a plan to remember the word.

3. Have students each share a sentence that relates to their life and their plan for remembering the target word.

4. Ask students to copy the word train into their notebook.

Independent Practice

Pair students with a partner for repeated practice of Word Train.

1. Distribute seven index cards to everyone and provide writing utensils, as needed.

2. Tell students that they will work independently at first, each choosing a study word and creating a train with as much information as they can.

3. Explain that after they complete their train, they will share their work orally with their partner and talk about links to their own lives based on the information on their word train.

4. Ask students to copy the word train they created into their notebook. They may also copy their partner's word train into their notebook, replacing their own link for remembering the word with their partner's.

5. Display the word trains in the classroom.

Stretching Students' Learning

◎   Discuss the target vocabulary words in relation to characters, settings, and themes being studied to enhance comprehension and oral and written expression.

report

export

Branching Out

Activity Overview

Having a well-developed vocabulary is essential to proficient reading comprehension. Various instructional strategies can help students learn words more efficiently and effectively. Networking related words, developing word consciousness, and linking words to the students' personal lives all encourage word learning.

Branching Out is an activity that emphasizes learning words in relationship to one another. When words are learned in groups, information networks are formed. These chunks of information are then stored in memory, creating neural networks with other words, ideas, and concepts—thus enabling the brain to more easily recall and retrieve the word.

Materials • • • • • • •

- ☺ Branching Out Worksheet (see Appendix A)
- ☺ Butcher paper, marker, and tape (*optional*)
- ☺ Plastic sheet protectors

Whole Classroom Instruction

Set the purpose. Say: "This activity will help you learn words in relation to other words. Learning words that are related makes them easier to understand, remember, and use."

1. Draw a tree on the front board with branches that can hold words related to the target word, prefix, suffix, or root.

2. Choose a target vocabulary word or root and write it in the trunk of the tree. Let's use the word *vehicle* as an example.

3. Generate ideas from the class of words related to *vehicle*: *bicycle, motorcycle, unicycle, tricycle, car, truck,* etc. The words can be written on sticky notes and placed on the branches. Then, when the students become familiar with the activity, they can generate ideas, write them on sticky notes, and bring them up one at a time to place them on the tree.

4. Use each word that is generated in a sentence orally and encourage students to make a mental image of the word. For instance: "The clown balanced himself carefully on the one big wheel of the **unicycle** he was riding."

   ↻ As an alternate strategy, Branching Out also works well as a word wall. Draw a tree on butcher paper. Have students add words to the branches and then surround the tree with the students' individual branching-out work.

Return to the purpose. Say: "Learning words that are related makes them easier to understand, remember, and use. This activity gives you practice in learning words that are related to each other."

Small Group Work

Students add words to the word tree based on the root "port."

1. Distribute Branching Out Worksheets and plastic sheet protectors.

2. Explain that the group work will work together on a new target vocabulary word, following the model that was made with the whole class.

3. Select a new target word and have students write the word on the trunk of the tree on their worksheet.

4. Generate ideas from the group for the branch words, which will all relate to the target word. Have students write the group's responses on their own worksheet.

5. Have students turn the Branching Out Worksheet over, draw a quick sketch that will help them remember the target word, and write a sentence using the word that creates a mental image for the reader.

6. Ask students to share a sentence that relates to their life and their plan for remembering the target word.

7. Tell students to put their worksheet into the sheet protector and place it in their notebook.

   ☺ As a variation, the Branching Out Worksheet can be used in a similar manner to the Word Train Worksheet, putting information about the word on the various branches of the tree: the definition; a picture of the word; a sentence using the word; information about the word (number of syllables, origin, morphemes, etc.); related words; and a link—a plan for remembering the word.

Independent Practice

Students will work in pairs this time to complete their individual Branching Out Worksheet.

1. Give students a list of target words or roots, another Branching Out Worksheet, and a plastic sheet protector.

2. Have them work together now to choose a word and complete their worksheet cooperatively. (The amount of collaborative support will very depending on the needs of students.)

3. Ask students to place their worksheet into their notebook when finished and share with their partner their plan for remembering the word.

4. Display some of the Branching Out Worksheets on a word wall in the classroom.

Stretching Students' Learning

⊚ Relate the words to characters, setting, and themes being studied to enhance comprehension and oral and written expression.

Schoolwide Vocabulary

Activity Overview

For students to be proficient at reading comprehension, they must have many exposures to words as part of their oral language and vocabulary instruction. Schoolwide Vocabulary is a simple, yet fun and effective way for students to increase their word consciousness and their mastery over words.

This is an activity in which every member of the school community participates by working on vocabulary words that are targeted for all-school, high-utility word learning. The words that are chosen should have significance to concepts taught in the classroom as well as to citizenship and achievement goals that will enhance the entire schoolwide community and climate. Words have power. Choosing words carefully can help support schoolwide goals. For example, different grade levels can take turns choosing important words. Citizenship words might include *responsibility*, *citizen*, *courteous*, *respectful*, and *generous*.

Materials ● ● ● ● ● ●

- ◎ Materials to make a large chart
- ◎ Photocopies (8 1/2⊠ by 11⊠) of the chart and tape
- ◎ Name badges (the clear, plastic type used at conferences, if available) or index cards and string for making badges
- ◎ Bulletin board and pins
- ◎ Balloons, blowers, noisemakers, and other items used in celebrations

Schoolwide Activity

Set the purpose. Say: "Words become known and understood the more chances you have to see them, hear them, and use them."

This activity is appropriate for all grade levels. The only difference would be the level of word study.

1. **Words in Action Assembly.** Schedule an assembly during which the principal announces that the whole school will start a vocabulary study project because vocabulary development is a value shared by everyone at the school.

   - ☻ The principal will explain that the goal of the schoolwide program is word consciousness in addition to word learning.

   - ☻ A system of schoolwide vocabulary points can be discussed. Students could earn points for learning the target words as well as for noticing the target words in a variety of settings outside of the homeroom or English classroom. For instance, if a student reports to his homeroom or English teacher (whatever makes the most sense) that the gym teacher used a specific word, the student gets a vocabulary point. If the whole class comes back and reports that they heard the word used in gym, then the whole class will get a vocabulary point. Keep track of points in a manner that best suits your school.

- ☺ The principal will also explain that as schoolwide vocabulary grows, schoolwide celebrations will be planned.
- ☺ Invite the athletic staff, librarian, kitchen staff, bus drivers, teachers, paraprofessionals, and office staff to participate in making the assembly engaging and entertaining for students. For example, the kitchen staff could state a word related to the job they perform (such as *spatula*), define it, and bring the object that illustrates the word. Others could put on word skits ("Words in Action") involving playing charades, whereby the entire assembly could be engaged in trying to figure out the words being acted out.

2. **Target Word Chart.** Place a chart of about five target words in the front hall of the school so students, parents, visitors, and the entire school community will see the words as soon as they enter the building. This list can be changed periodically (e.g., weekly) depending on your students' needs. Make photocopies of the chart to disseminate.
   - ☺ Post a copy of the chart in every classroom, the lunch room, the teacher's work room, the library, the gym, the music and art rooms, and on all buses.
   - ☺ Send a copy of the chart home to all parents, day-care providers, and after-school programs directors and teachers.
   - ☺ Give every student a copy of the chart to tape to their desks.

3. **Wear a Word.** Ask all school administrators, staff, teachers, and visitors to wear a word badge (name badge) that contains one of the target words (see the Wear a Word activity in the Fluency section for more specific directions). Therefore, when students go to gym class, the gym teacher will be wearing a word badge, she will use the word she is wearing several times during the class, and she will have posted the target words.

4. **How Well Do I Know It?—Bulletin Board.** Put up a bulletin board in the front hall of the school that is similar to the one discussed in How Well Do I Know It? earlier in this Vocabulary section. It will have three categories of words: Unknown, Known, and Own.
   - ☺ All new words that the school will work on will start out in the Unknown category.
   - ☺ Each teacher will report on her class's progress in word learning. As classes learn words, the words will be moved to the Known and Own categories. Individual schools can determine how this will be decided.
   - ☺ As the school year proceeds, everyone will be able to measure their school's vocabulary growth by looking at the number of words that started out in the Unknown category and now are listed in the Known and Own categories. Different grade levels can share

responsibility for maintaining the bulletin board. You will have created a bar graph of student word knowledge.

5. **Schoolwide Celebrations.** Plan short-term rewards for the development of word consciousness as students accumulate vocabulary points. Then choose logical points at which to have "Words in Action" assemblies and celebrations. Invite the entire school staff to participate in the celebrations.

    ℮ Have a "Words in Action" parade where students dress up like words.

    ℮ Give students balloons on which they write one of the vocabulary words they have studied. They will inflate the balloon in homeroom and enter the assembly holding their balloon.

    ℮ Give students blowers and noisemakers and have each class stand up and cheer for a particular word when it is announced.

Comprehension
～∘～ Activities ～∘～

41. Picture Perfect Notes
42. Links to My Life
43. Coding for Concepts
44. Thinking in Pictures
45. The Comprehension Train
46. Growing Sentences
47. What's In the Bucket?
48. Sentence Mix-Ups
49. Picturing the Story
50. Living Concept Maps

Direct instruction in comprehension with opportunities for modeling, guided feedback, and independent practice can improve students' ability to understand both narrative and expository text. Research on the key factors that impact comprehension include the characteristics of the reader, the nature of the text, and the characteristics of the reading task in which students are engaged. Some examples of these factors follow.

The Characteristics of the Reader

- ◎ Phonological decoding skills and word recognition skills
- ◎ Oral language abilities, including vocabulary
- ◎ Short-term and working memory abilities
- ◎ Background knowledge
- ◎ Ability to link new learning with previous learning
- ◎ Ability to attend to the text, stay engaged, and respond to the text

The Nature of the Text

- ◎ Narrative versus expository
- ◎ Unknown vocabulary
- ◎ Sentence complexity
- ◎ Organization of text (graphics, subtitles, etc.)
- ◎ Clarity and cohesion of the writing

Comprehension Activities

Characteristics of the Reading Task

- ⦿ The purpose of the reading task

- ⦿ The degree of structure of the assignment

- ⦿ The time limit provided

- ⦿ Scaffolding and accommodations based on skill level

Because various complex factors influence reading comprehension, it is important that teachers get to the root cause of why students have difficulty understanding text. For students who have problems decoding and reading words, the phonemic awareness and word study sections in this book can help boost their comprehension. If students' word knowledge is limited, then the vocabulary activities in this book will be beneficial.

The activities in this section deal primarily with text comprehension and the link between oral language comprehension and text comprehension. The activities will help students use words that they know and words they are learning, make mental pictures that are connected to what they are reading, and learn to connect new information to their past experiences and background knowledge.

The Four Processing Systems Connection

This activity emphasizes the meaning and context processor of the reading brain. However, in order to read vocabulary the student must be able to decode the word. The student needs to know the sound/symbol connection, which engages both the phonological and orthographic processors, while at the same time know the meaning of the words and be able to use the owned word in the context of a sentence, which engages the meaning and connect processors.

Knowing word meanings alone is not enough. For deep comprehension, students must be able to connect new learning to background knowledge and use and understand words within the structure of more complex sentences, passages, and narrative and expository text. Therefore, the context processor takes center stage when addressing activities that enhance reading comprehension.

The Assessment Connection

- ⦿ *DIBELS: Dynamic Indicators of Basic Early Literacy Skills.* Word Use Fluency: Provides an indicator of students' vocabulary knowledge and level of expressive language skills.

- ⦿ *DIBELS: Dynamic Indicators of Basic Early Literacy Skills.* Oral Reading Fluency: Measures whether students can read connected text accurately and fluently.

- ⦿ *DIBELS: Dynamic Indicators of Basic Early Literacy Skills.* Retell Fluency: Measures students' ability to tell about what was read in the Oral Reading Fluency passage. Identifies students who can read accurately and with speed but who do not comprehend or remember what was read.

The ELL Connection

Many of the activities in this section will be effective with ELLs without any alteration. However, a few small changes can have a great impact on the achievement and skill development for these students. The following are a few ideas to try that may enhance the effectiveness of the comprehension activities:

- ⦿ These activities all can be used in the students' first language and then transitioned into use with English instruction.

◎ Preview content for ELLs in a small group before covering the content with the entire class. Doing so will give ELL students a "heads-up." The whole-class activity will be their second exposure to the material, and a brief third exposure will occur when you check for comprehension later and look for any information the students might not have understood.

◎ Making connections to one's life and then illustrating the connections deepens language comprehension.

◎ Create opportunities for students to share connections orally to enhance oral language skill development.

◎ Use basic retelling words (*who, what, where, when,* and *why*) to help students structure their conversations.

◎ Teaching sentence grammar with opportunities for discussion and practice is important for students who are learning English as a second language. Multi-sensory sentence grammar (e.g., physically moving the parts of a sentence) and coding sentences will help students understand syntax that may be different.

◎ Combining sentence construction with acting out can help check for understanding.

◎ Graphic organizers help students organize their thoughts for expressing themselves orally and in writing. These tools can be especially useful for ELL students.

◎ Group and partner work provides modeling for oral language that is helpful to ELLs. In addition, the small group and partner settings offer environments that encourage more risk taking in the area of oral language.

Dig In to Learn More

Beck, I.L., McKeown, M.G., Hamilton, R.I., & Kucan, I. (Eds.) (1997). *Questioning the author: An approach for enhancing student engagement with text*. Newark, DE: International Reading Association.

Moats, L. C. (2005). *Language essentials for teachers of reading and spelling (LETRS), Module 6—Digging for meaning: Teaching text comprehension*. Longmont, CO: Sopris West Educational Services.

Moats, L. C., & Sedita, J. (2006). *Language essentials for teachers of reading and spelling (LETRS), Module 11—Writing: A road to reading comprehension*. Longmont, CO: Sopris West Educational Services.

National Reading Panel. (1999). *Teaching children to read: An evidence-based assessment of the scientific research on reading and its implications for reading instruction*. National Reading Panel Publications (www.nationalreadingpanel.org/Publications/publications.htm).

Comprehension Activities

Picture Perfect Notes

Activity Overview

Creating mental pictures is a critical comprehension strategy that enables deeper understanding of text. Good readers make pictures in their minds as they read. When students read without making pictures, their understanding is tied to what they can remember about the words they have read. When students make mental pictures, they can then refer back to their pictures as a source of reference for comprehension as well as for recalling the words and concepts.

Picture Perfect Notes is an activity that incorporates the use of pictures added to note taking to support understanding, recall, and retrieval of important facts and concepts that have been read. It teaches the difference between note taking and note making, as students go back to their original notes and add color, pictures, and highlight important facts to aid in recall and understanding.

We don't have to think of note taking and note making activities as appropriate only for older students. This activity gets students of a young age to connect with what they are reading and to develop habits of focusing on what is important. By starting students young in simple ways with only a few key words and more pictures, you can guide them to become automatic with these important skills.

Materials

- Transparency and student copies of a familiar, short nonfiction passage
- Overhead projector and two colors of pens
- Transparency of a three-column note page
- Highlighters in two colors for students
- Transparency of an unfamiliar short passage
- Student copies of three-column note page
- Student copies of a familiar reading passage
- Whiteboard (or chart paper), dry-erase marker, and eraser
- Student whiteboards, dry-eraser markers, and erasers
- Plastic sheet protectors
- Student copies of a partially completed note page
- Colored pens or pencils

Whole Classroom Instruction

Set the purpose. Say: "Making pictures in your mind helps you remember and understand what you read. In this activity, you will learn to incorporate pictures as you take notes about your reading."

This activity can be done with all grade levels and provides a valuable link between reading, recall, and verbalizing about what has been read. It is important to go slowly enough so that students have many opportunities to practice in a supported environment.

Comprehension

1. Place a short nonfiction passage on an overhead projector. Begin with something you have already read and discussed so that the students have adequate background knowledge to understand the piece.

2. Give each student a copy of the passage so that they have it in front of them as you read.

3. Read the passage aloud and quickly review the main idea and some of the details in the passage. Have students use their own markers to work along with you as you use one color to mark the main idea in the passage and another color to mark some of the details.

4. Remove the passage and put a transparency of the three-column note page on the overhead projector. Label columns "Main Idea," "Pictures," and "Details."

    ☞ Write in the main idea in the left column.

    ☞ Guide the class to look at the passage and what you highlighted together, and ask them to help come up with the details for the right column.

    ☞ After coming up with the details, draw a couple of quick pictures in the center column that will help you recall the details and the main idea.

Animal Habitat

Main Idea	Pictures	Details
forest animals		live in caves, dens, bushes, holes

☞ After completing the notes, model summarizing what has been learned by reading the notes, starting with the main idea, and adding the details, ending with a closing statement about the topic. This creates a model of paragraph writing: topic sentence (main idea), detail sentences, ending with a closing sentence. For example:

There are many different animals that live in the forest. Foxes can be found in many forests. They live in caves, dens, bushes, and holes. Foxes hunt and eat smaller animals. Summary: The forest provides food and shelter for foxes and other animals that make the forest their home.

5. After students appear comfortable with the process, repeat it using unfamiliar text.

6. Place a short, unfamiliar passage on the overhead projector and give a copy to students. Preview the passage, building background knowledge as needed. Read it aloud to the class, and then proceed with the same steps as before.

Return to the purpose. Say: "Using pictures with your notes will help you understand text better and will also help you remember the reading when you review the notes."

Small Group Work

Use familiar passages when possible for this activity to ensure background knowledge.

1. Distribute a copy of a familiar passage to students.

2. Use a whiteboard to introduce the concept (subskill) of abbreviations such as *lb., oz.,* state abbreviations, and months of the year.

3. Have students practice using abbreviations on their whiteboards. For example, space shuttle = SS, because = b/c.

4. Next, ask students to choose three words from the passage and make up abbreviations for those words, writing them on their whiteboards. Then have them all teach the new abbreviations they have come up with to each other.

5. Have students create a three-column note page by dividing a blank page into three columns. Have students label the columns "Main Idea," "Pictures," and "Details."

6. Tell students to use their three-column note page to take notes on the passage using the abbreviations incorporated into the notes. Be sure they include main idea, pictures, and details.

7. Have students share their notes with one another then summarize their notes orally.

8. For emphasis, repeat this procedure with other important subskills such as the use of notations like stars, asterisks, and arrows for emphasis. Follow the same procedure and then have students share their notes.

This student works to complete three-column notes.

Independent Practice

Have students work in pairs for this portion of the activity.

1. Give each student a copy of a reading passage in a sheet protector, paper with which to make a three-column note page, and a partially completed note page from one of the lessons you modeled previously. Provide colored pens or pencils as needed.

2. Ask partners to begin together to figure out the main idea first.

3. Review the instructions for completing their three-column notes (main idea, picture, and details that illustrate the concepts), and have them work together to finish taking three-column notes.

Stretching Students' Learning

◉ Increase the length and complexity of the text to be read and deconstructed into notes.

◉ Follow oral summarization of notes by having students write their summary.

Links to My Life

Activity Overview

Linking information is an effective comprehension strategy for deepening learning and making the new information more accessible for recall. Links to My Life is an activity that helps students think about how their own life is linked to words, concepts, and ideas they are learning about. By connecting new learning with previous knowledge, the new knowledge is more easily understood, retained, and retrieved.

Materials • • • • • • • •

- Sticky notes
- Whiteboard, dry-erase marker, and eraser
- Links to My Life Worksheet (see Appendix A)
- Word Chain Worksheet (see Appendix A)
- Chart paper

Whole Classroom Instruction

Set the purpose. Say: "Linking what you are learning to your own life can help you learn faster and remember better. This activity will give you practice connecting information you are learning to your own life and the world around you."

1. Read a short text from a book to the class.

2. As you read, stop when appropriate, and think aloud about the connections that you can make to your own life, other stories you have heard or read, other people, the community or the world.

   - When you make a connection, take a sticky note and put it on the page that made you think of the link to your life.

3. When you have finished reading, draw three or four chain links on the whiteboard.

4. Using the book, turn to the first sticky note. Reread the section and ask if anyone can recall what you said your link was to that passage of the text. The person who remembers earns reading points that can be accumulated and put toward rewards.

5. Write a note in the first chain about your link to the text.

6. Repeat this process, moving through the sticky notes quickly.

7. Ask if anyone else in the class has made a link to their life and if they would like to share that link.

Return to the purpose. Say: "Linking what you are learning to your own life can help you learn faster and remember better. In this activity, you will have practice connecting new information to your own life and the world around you."

Small Group Work

1. Distribute a copy of the Word Chain Worksheet (used earlier in the Language Links activity) to everyone.

2. Read a short passage to the students. Ask the group to listen and think about links they can make to the passage as you read.

3. Reread the passage and this time have students share their own links as they listen. Do this so that each student makes at least one link.

4. Record the students' links on a piece of chart paper.

5. Have students copy some of the links onto their worksheet.

This student is reading for a purpose and marking a page with a sticky note.

Independent Practice

This portion of the activity involves both independent and partner work.

1. Distribute copies of the Links to My Life Worksheet to everyone.

2. Using the same Word Chain Worksheet from their small group work, ask students to choose one link to illustrate.

3. On their Links to My Life Worksheet, have students write their link at the top of the page and then draw their illustration of the link using colored pens or pencils.

4. When they finish, tell students to share their link and illustration with their partner.
   - Have students use the basic retelling words (*who, what, where, when,* and *why*) to help support their sharing conversation.

Stretching Students' Learning

- Use both narrative and expository texts of increasingly complex levels. For example, if students are learning about Africa, they would look for the connections with their own lives and previously learned information rather than just gathering information.

Coding for Concepts

Activity Overview

Students enjoy being language detectives. They think of the English language as a code, and their job is to crack that code to get a deeper understanding into what makes it work. Coding for Concepts builds on that enjoyment and sense of accomplishment when another piece of the code is demystified and clarified.

Reading comprehension skills are tied to oral language skills. Sometimes when students have weak reading comprehension at the story or passage level, it makes sense to go back and explore the sentence-level comprehension with them. Sentences have a code of their own, and this activity builds a simple way for students to explore and master the code of sentences.

Most children gain knowledge of sentence structure by listening to spoken language in their families and communities. However, the structure of academic texts and other reading material that students encounter in and out of school may be less familiar and may bring extra challenges in terms of comprehension. Good readers and writers are aware of sentence structure. They can construct and deconstruct sentences, move words around, and manipulate the words to get their ideas expressed in a way they think is best. Weaker readers have difficulty constructing sentences and may also misconstrue what they read. Direct instruction in written sentence structure, with opportunities for practice, can increase students' ability to comprehend written material.

Materials • • • • • • •

- Whiteboard, dry-erase markers, and eraser
- Magnifying glass (*optional*)
- Student whiteboards, dry-erase markers, and erasers (or pencil and paper)
- Chart paper
- Large sticky notes
- Reading passages placed in plastic sheet protectors
- Sentence Coding Worksheet (see Appendix A)

Whole Classroom Instruction

Set the purpose. Say: "The English language has a code. You have already learned about the code of sounds and letters. Today you will be learning about the code of sentences. In this activity, you will be looking for clues to the code. Learning about the code of sentences will help you understand the sentences you read better and write sentences more easily."

1. Teach a part of the sentence code. For instance: "Every sentence has a subject and predicate. The subject refers to who or what the sentence is about. The predicate refers to what that person or thing is doing or was doing."

2. Write a sentence on the whiteboard. Model for students as you read the sentence and think aloud about who or what the sentence is about: **"Danny plays his guitar."**

   ↻ Explain that you think the sentence is about **Danny,** so you have found your first clue.

- ℮ If you have a magnifying glass, hold it up to the sentence and place it over the word *Danny*.
- ℮ With a colored marker, draw a box around the word *Danny*: [Danny] **plays his guitar.** Say, **"Danny** is the subject of the sentence."

3. Ask students what they think Danny is doing. They will say he plays his guitar. Explain that "plays his guitar" must therefore be the predicate of the sentence. Draw a line under the words *plays his guitar*: [Danny] **plays his guitar.**

Cracking the Code of Sentence Grammar

You can make up your own methods for coding a sentence or have your class come up with them. You may post the code on a sentence grammar bulletin board with a key like the one that follows.

Subject = who or what	Code = put a box around it	Example: [Our class] loves to read.
Predicate = is doing or was doing	Code = put a line under it	Example: [Our class] loves to read.

---

4. Now write another sentence on the whiteboard and have students copy the sentence onto their whiteboards. For example: **Ana rides her gray horse.**
   - ℮ This time work with students asking what is the subject (who is it about?) and what is the predicate (what is the person doing?). Have the students code the answers using the box and an underline: [Ana] **rides her gray horse.**

5. Repeat this process with several sentences, adding on other concepts only after they have been taught explicitly.

Return to the purpose. Say: "Cracking the code of sentences will make you better readers and writers."

Small Group Work

1. As a group have students create a few sentences while you write them on a whiteboard.

2. Copy the first one onto chart paper. For example: **My dog likes to hide bones**.

3. Work together to decide who the first sentence is about and what the person or thing is doing. Code the first sentence for students.

4. Have students copy the second sentence onto their whiteboards and then code it by putting a box around the subject and underlining the predicate.
   - ℮ Check their answers as a group when everyone has finished.

5. Repeat this procedure with each sentence that was created.

6. Next, give students large sticky notes and have them deconstruct one of the sentences by writing the subject on one sticky note and the predicate on another.

Comprehension

Talking Classroom

7. Have students reread the sentences, segmenting them into subject and predicate, and then reconstruct them and read normally.

Independent Practice

Have students work in pairs for this portion of the activity.

1. Give students a short passage at their independent reading level, placed in a plastic sheet protector, and a Sentence Coding Worksheet.

2. Tell students to use a dry-erase marker to code three of the sentences in the paragraph for subject and predicate.

3. Ask students to read their sentences to each other and explain why they made their decisions to code the sentences in the way they did. For instance: 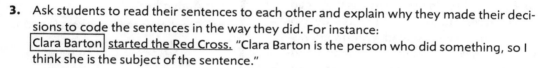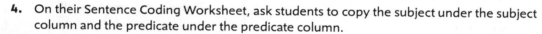Clara Barton started the Red Cross. "Clara Barton is the person who did something, so I think she is the subject of the sentence."

4. On their Sentence Coding Worksheet, ask students to copy the subject under the subject column and the predicate under the predicate column.

Stretching Students' Learning

◎ Increase the length and complexity of the sentences to be read and deconstructed.

◎ The Sentence Coding Worksheet can be differentiated for more advanced students, using columns to code for nouns, verbs, adjectives, and adverbs.

Thinking in Pictures

Activity Overview

Creating mental pictures is a foundational comprehension strategy. Good readers make pictures in their minds as they read and can then refer to these pictures as they think about what they have just read. When students read without making pictures, their understanding is limited to what they can remember about the words. When students make pictures in their mind, they can then refer back to their pictures as a source of reference and support for comprehension. Thinking in Pictures reinforces the use of pictures to enhance students' understanding of text that they have read.

Materials • • • • • •

- Thinking in Pictures Worksheet (see Appendix A)
- Chart paper and markers (*optional*)
- Retelling Words List (see Appendix A)
- Paper and colored pencils
- Passages of text for reading

Whole Classroom Instruction

Set the purpose. Say: "Making pictures in your mind can help you to understand and remember what you read. Thinking in Pictures is an activity that will help you to make mental pictures of words, characters, and ideas in the stories that you listen to and read."

1. Choose a short story or expository text to read aloud.

Sample Expository Text

Did you know that some fish can fly? It is true! They do not really fly like birds. But some fish can glide through the air. These fish are called flying fish. They have long fins on either side of their bodies. When a flying fish leaves the water, it spreads its fins. The air catches under the fins. The air under the fins helps the fish glide. Flying fish can glide at speeds of 40 miles per hour. They can go as far as 30 meters before they splash down.

Excerpt taken from *The Six-Minute Solution: A Reading Fluency Program*, by G. Adams and S. Brown, 2007, Longmont, CO Sopris West Educational Services.

2. Introduce the notion of picturing the ideas in the story, and then read your selected text to the class.

Comprehension

3. Use short passages at first and introduce the concept of retelling words (see the following suggested list—you can also create your own retelling word list depending on your students' ability level). These are words that help students make mental pictures that they can discuss when they are asked to remember information from a passage or story. Ask students to consider just a few words as they begin practicing retelling stories and recalling information from text. Build up slowly to their ability to consider all of the words as they listen, recall, and retell.

Retelling Words

1. who
2. what
3. where
4. when
5. why

6. size
7. color
8. sound
9. texture
10. feelings

4. Create a Thinking in Pictures chart on the front board or chart paper. Create some quick sketches based on words, ideas, or characters in the text you have read.

Thinking in Pictures

Word, Idea, or Character	Visualize It
flying fish	
glide	

5. Ask the class to help you generate ideas for what you should put in the pictures on the chart. Explain that these pictures will give the basic idea but should also contain enough detail to help you recall information when going back to look at the pictures.

   ☞ Model that you are thinking about some of the retelling words. Say, "Can you tell how big the fins are? Can I add color? What about texture? Can you hear the fish jumping? Is the glider quiet or noisy?"

6. Go back to the sketches with the class and check to see if they can recall who, what, where, when, size, feeling, and so on as you look at your sketches.

Return to the purpose. Say: "Making pictures in your mind helps you to understand what you read. This activity gives you practice using your mental pictures to recall words, ideas, and characters when you listen and read."

Small Group Work

1. Choose a text for your read-aloud.

2. Read the text and then distribute a Thinking in Pictures chart, a copy of the Retelling Words List, paper, and colored pencils.

3. Ask the group to choose a word or idea from the text to visualize and draw. Have everyone write that word or idea and draw a sketch on their chart to go along with it.

4. Guide the group to talk about the pictures, being sure to use the retelling words to help structure the discussion.

Independent Practice

Have students work with a partner for more practice. This is not primarily an art activity—the creation of quick pictures that represent images derived while reading is the focus. Drawing detailed pictures based on the text read is a valuable activity but one that should not be done during reading instruction. It can be included in a long-term project, a homework assignment, or as part of a collaborative learning activity.

1. Give everyone a Thinking in Pictures Worksheet and each set of partners a carefully selected text that is within their independent reading level.

2. Tell partners to read the text carefully and to complete the Thinking in Pictures Worksheet when they finish.

   ℗ Partners can make decisions independently about what they will illustrate.

Stretching Students' Learning

◎ Increase the length and complexity of the text to be read and visualized.

◎ For students who are ready for more challenges, have them take a new passage or story, read it, create images, and then write a summary of the story (see Picture Perfect Notes for more ideas).

Comprehension Train

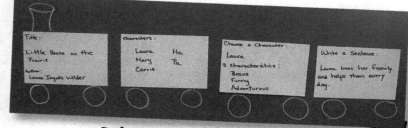

Activity Overview

When students have a structured way of organizing the information they are reading, they are more likely to understand and connect to the information, thus helping them to retain and retell what they have learned. In this activity, students choose specific aspects of a story or topic they have read and then explain, define, draw, write, and network connections in a simple and clear manner.

Materials

- Index cards with magnetic tape on the back (or large sticky notes) (*optional*)
- Paper (*optional*)
- Index cards for students
- Pencils, colored pencils, markers, and/or crayons
- Copies of familiar stories

Whole Classroom Instruction

Set the purpose. Say: "Knowing how to organize information you are learning can help you understand and remember the information better. This activity will give you practice organizing new information and connecting it to things you already know, making it easier to talk about what you have learned."

This activity is appropriate for all grade levels. A first grader might build his train based on decodable text, forest habitat, or a read-aloud book. A fifth grader might do a character study for a novel she is reading. A ninth-grade student might use this activity to study the factors that contributed to the Industrial Revolution.

1. Model building a word train on the front board using a story you have all been reading or listening to or a theme of study in any content area. Draw some boxes and fill them in to represent the cars of the train, or use index cards with magnetic tape on the back. (Modeling can also be done on the floor using pieces of paper to build the train with students seated in a circle on the floor.)

   Car #1. Write the name of the book or a theme, for instance, *The Little House on the Prairie* by Laura Ingalls Wilder.

   Car #2. Write a character's name, such as Laura, and draw a quick sketch of Laura.

   Car #3. List one characteristic of Laura that you think is important, such as courage. Ask the class if they can think of a time in the book when Laura was *brave*. Write a sentence based on their memory of the story: "Laura was **brave** when she . . . "

   Car #4. Ask the class to think of another characteristic that describes Laura. Someone may come up with "funny," "kind," etc. Write the word, then let students think

of something that illustrates this characteristic. Write a sentence using that example.

2. Continue this until you have several card/cars on the train.

   ℮ Students should be able to look at the train and create a character study. For example: "Laura is brave, funny, and kind. I know she is brave because I remember when she saved her dog. I know she is funny because she loved to learn to spit with Mr. Edwards. I know she is kind because even though she is young, she cares about others."

   ℮ The sentences that you wrote as you were building the train make the retelling easy as the students look back and can go from the name to the detail to the sentence.

Return to the purpose. Say: "Organizing your thoughts about what you read and linking those thoughts to things you know helps you understand more and be able to share what you have learned."

Small Group Work

Note: The number of train cars can vary depending on students' abilities.

1. Guide students to follow the same train-building steps as taught during whole class instruction, this time working together using index cards.

2. Use a story that the class has read as a group. Have students begin by writing the title of the book on the first card/car.

3. Next, they should write the first detail about the story on the second card/car and make a quick sketch of it.

4. On the third card/car, ask students to write a sentence about that detail. Add another detail and, on the last car, ask them to write another sentence.

5. Have students share their work orally and then make one connection to their own life based on the content. For example: "I was once brave when . . ." Or, "My brother is funny when he tells jokes and does magic tricks."

   ℮ You can also have students use the cars to make a summary statement about the story. You will need to model this process for students.

Independent Practice

Have students work in pairs for this portion of the Comprehension Train.

1. Distribute index cards and copies of a familiar story to everyone.

2. Tell students to work independently, adding two or more card/cars to their comprehension train.

3. After completing their train, have students share their work orally with their partner and talk about links to their own lives based on the information they have included on their train.

4. Display the students' comprehension trains in the classroom.

Stretching Students' Learning

◉ Have students create well-written paragraphs in the content areas with both narrative and expository text to summarize what they have read and learned from the stories used in The Comprehension Train activity.

Comprehension Comprehension Train

Growing Sentences

Activity Overview

O ral language skills put down the foundation for reading comprehension. A key to developing and improving oral language skills involves direct instruction in the code of sentence structure combined with opportunities to create sentences for speaking and writing. This activity helps students use words to describe other words and ideas while giving practice in listening to, creating, and writing complete sentences.

Growing Sentences presents students with sentence starters in the form of sentence "stems" from which bigger sentences can grow. Using the structure of sentence stems increases the possibility that, when students are ready, they will be able to adapt the given structure to their own needs, first transferring the routine and finally adapting it to become their own.

Materials • • • • • • •

- ◎ Koosh ball*
- ◎ Chart paper and marker
- ◎ Sentence Stem Worksheet (see Appendix A)
- ◎ Colored pencils (or markers)

* Available in the optional Classroom Manipulatives Kit

Whole Classroom Instruction

Set the purpose. Say: "This activity provides practice in building sentences. We will start with the basics of sentence building using a beginning idea called a stem. You will learn to grow your sentences, just like flowers that get bigger and prettier as they grow upon their stem."

1. Write a sentence stem on the board. It should be something that you know will have meaning for your students. Depending on the level of your students, it can be quite simple or more complex. For example:

   Level A: I like to eat . . .
   Level B: If I could have any wish, it would be . . .

2. Create one response yourself, such as: "I like to eat **mint chocolate chip ice cream**." Be sure to repeat the sentence as a whole, modeling not just the ending but the entire sentence in a fluent manner.

3. Have students turn to a neighbor and share how they would end the sentence, then repeat the whole sentence with their personal ending.

4. Ask students to get up and move around the room. Explain that when you give a signal to stop, they will share their sentence ending and repeat the whole sentence to the person they stop near. Both people will share their sentences.

5. Tell students to move on to another person, and this time have them share their own sentence ending and the sentence of the last person who they were speaking with.

Return to the purpose. Say: "When you can say bigger and better sentences, it will make it easier for you to understand them when you listen and read. This activity gives you practice in building sentences from a sentence stem."

Small Group Work

1. Explain that you will provide a sentence stem and that they are going to build sentences— one word or phrase at a time—as they toss the Koosh ball to each other.

    ☺ As a student tosses the ball to a classmate, the student will add a word or phrase to the sentence that has been started. Each person has to say the words that were said before his turn and then add his words to the sentence. He will then repeat the whole sentence as it is up to that point.

    ☺ For students who have difficulty with sentence construction, start with a sentence stem about something the class knows and cares about. For instance, if you have been study-ing Native Americans, you may have a sentence that starts with: "The Plains Indians liked to . . ." Or, "Some woodland animals eat . . ."

2. Toss the Koosh ball to the first student, state the sentence stem ("If I had one wish, I would like . . ."), and ask the student to add one word or phrase to the sentence.

    ☺ The student then tosses the ball to a classmate, repeats the sentence so far, then adds her own words: "If I had one wish, I would like **no child to be hungry.**"

    ☺ The entire group repeats the sentence chorally.

3. Write the sentence on a piece of chart paper for review later.

4. Begin the activity again with the same sentence starter so that more people get to partici-pate. Whenever it is appropriate, change the sentence starter and begin again.

Independent Practice

Have students work with a partner for more practice building sentences.

1. Distribute a copy of the Sentence Stem Worksheet and colored pencils to everyone.

2. Have students choose a sentence that they built from sentence stems during Small Group work and copy it down on their Sentence Stem Worksheet.

3. Tell students to share their sentence with their partner.

4. Instruct students to illustrate their sentence and then share their illustration with their partner.

5. This activity can be repeated depending on the amount of time that is available.

What's In the Bucket?*

Activity Overview

What's In the Bucket? helps students develop the comprehension skills necessary for identifying and naming the main idea of what they read. Comprehending is partly dependent on getting the gist of what one reads, or chunking information. Some students seem to be able to organize information automatically while others need support and direct instruction in order to do that.

Identifying the main idea of a passage involves finding an overarching category or topic. For students to identify the main idea, they need to be able to compare and contrast the details, looking for a common thread. Whether looking for categories from simple lists or reading a multiparagraph expository text, students must identify the details, compare those details for what they have in common, and then paraphrase them or translate them into a larger theme or category.

Materials ● ● ● ● ● ● ●

- ◎ Index cards and marker for making word cards
- ◎ Whiteboard, dry-erase marker, and eraser
- ◎ Bucket
- ◎ Pieces of string
- ◎ List of words that relate to a topic or theme being taught
- ◎ Student whiteboards, dry-erase markers, and erasers
- ◎ Chart paper and marker
- ◎ What's In the Bucket? Worksheet (see Appendix A)
- ◎ Sticky notes
- ◎ Clip art pictures (*optional*)

Whole Classroom Instruction

Set the purpose. Say: "Today you are going to practice finding the main idea of what you read. Being able to identify the main idea will help you understand what you are reading."

Prior to introducing What's In the Bucket? choose a main topic (overarching category) from your reading or a unit of study and make word cards (details/categories) to go along with that topic. For example, a main topic could be *Native Americans*; subcategories might include *houses*, *food*, *culture*, and *tribes*; and supporting details might include *buffalo, Cheyenne, teepees,* and *spirits*.

This activity can be done at any grade level, varying the complexity but still working on getting students to identify the main idea.

1. Give one word card to each student, including the one card that has the main idea.

2. Have students walk around the room with their word card, holding their card so they can easily read each others'. Some of the cards have the main idea and subcategories on them, and the rest are details that fall under the subcategories.

*Adapted from the work of Joan Sedita, *LETRS* Module 11

3. Explain that students are to make judgments about where they belong based on how their card relates to the other words they see as they walk around. When they think they have found their "group," they stand with those other students. After students have found their group, have them read their cards aloud to the others in the group.

4. Next, tell the groups to decide whether someone in their group has a card with the main idea. If someone does, then that person with the main idea gets to sit in a chair in the middle of the room.

Students place their cards in the bucket.

5. Hand a bucket to the student in the chair and have all the other students stand around the main bucket in their subcategory groups. For example, if the main idea is *grocery store*, then *fresh produce, bakery, meat, canned goods, deli, florist*, and other related terms would all be secondary categories that go under the main idea.

6. Have students place their cards in the bucket and return to their seats. Next, you take the cards out of the bucket, one by one, and lay out the details under the category cards.

7. Have the class participate in developing a word wall. Give them pieces of string and tape with which to attach their card to the bucket.

Return to the purpose. Say: "You have been practicing finding the main idea and details that go along with the main idea. Identifying the main idea and the information that supports it will really help you understand what you're reading."

Small Group Work

1. Distribute a list of words that relates to a topic or theme being taught. For example: *sports* (main topic): *baseball, basketball, volleyball, lacrosse, stick, bat, ball, field, diamond, court.*

2. Have students work together to sort the words in terms of main idea and details.

3. Tell students to draw a bucket on their whiteboard and to write the detail words inside the bucket (or outside the bucket and connect them to the bucket with arrows).

Talking Classroom

4. Ask students to create sentences using the main idea and to include some details, such as **"Baseball** is a **sport** that is played with a **bat** and a **ball**."

5. Write the sentences on chart paper and tell the students to choose one to copy onto their whiteboards.

6. Have the group code the sentences that they wrote on their whiteboards by circling the main idea and boxing the details.

Independent Practice

Have students work with a partner for more practice with this activity.

1. Give students a What's In the Bucket? Worksheet and sticky notes.

2. Have students choose a topic from a selection of topics or they may choose something they are interested in.

3. Ask them to label the bucket with their topic (main idea).

4. Next, have students use sticky notes to write details (one per sticky note) about their topic and then add them to the bucket.

5. Tell students to each create a sentence about the main idea, which includes at least one detail, and orally rehearse the sentence with their partner.

6. After students have rehearsed their sentence, have them write the sentence at the bottom of their worksheet and code it by circling the main idea and boxing the details.

Stretching Students' Learning

- Increase the length and complexity of the text to be analyzed for the main idea.
- Have students find paragraph main ideas or chapter main ideas.

Sentence Mix-Ups

cat

the

Activity Overview

Sentence Mix-Ups lets students literally take the structure of a sentence and deconstruct it, making it into a puzzle that needs to be worked out. This activity is very enjoyable and challenging for students. It gives them a chance to be language detectives, whose job it is to crack the code of the English language. With probing questions and guidance, this activity also can give students meaningful opportunities to practice applying what they already know about the code of sentence structure in the English language.

Materials • • • • • • •

- Card stock and marker
- Chart paper (*optional*)
- Student whiteboards, dry-erase markers, and erasers
- Sentence strips
- Sticky notes

Whole Classroom Instruction

Set the purpose. Say: "This activity will give you practice building sentences by moving words around. Making sentences and then changing them can improve your ability to speak, read, and write."

1. Select a sentence from students' reading books and write each word on a separate piece of card stock. For example: **The—horse—galloped—through—the—meadow**.

2. Create a few extra cards with different verbs and adjectives to add flexibility. In the case of the example given, you might create extra cards that say **ran** and **quickly**, which could be added to the initial sentence.

3. Without telling the class what the sentence is, distribute the basic sentence cards to individual students and ask those students to come to the front of the room and hold their cards in front of them.

4. Ask the class to figure out a sentence from the mixed-up words, then have the students with the cards form that sentence.

5. Have everyone (including the students holding up the word cards) say the sentence together.

6. Ask questions about the sentence based on what has been previously taught. For example: "Who can tell me what this sentence is mostly about?" "Is that the subject or the predicate?" "What is the predicate of this sentence?" "Who can name the verb?"

7. Now, distribute the few extra cards showing verbs and adjectives.

8. Say the original sentence again, this time changing the word *ran* to *galloped*: "The horse **galloped** quickly through the meadow." Ask the student with a card that says *galloped* to join the sentence.

   ℮ As sentences are being created physically with the students, you can be writing them on the front board or on chart paper.

9. Have everyone say the new sentence.

10. Repeat the process of making one or two more changes.

Students work together to unscramble the sentence.

Return to the purpose. Say: "Sentence Mix-Ups gives you practice building sentences and then creating new sentences by moving the words around. By practicing making changes in sentences, you will improve your ability to speak, read, and write."

Small Group Work

1. Have the group copy a sentence from a text they are reading onto their whiteboards. For instance: "The boy and his friend came in when it started to rain."

2. Using that sentence as a base, have students read the sentence orally together. Check to be sure everyone understands what the sentence means.

3. Working at the oral level first, ask students to make one change to the sentence. Call on each student for a contribution. You might ask students to either change the noun, change the subject, add an adjective or verb, or change the simple subject to a more complete subject. A student adding an adjective might say, "The **tired** boy and his friend came in when it started to rain."

4. Have students say a simple sentence that you give them. Then ask them to say it again but with a particular change that you specify (a different subject, adding an adjective, etc.).

Independent Practice

Have students work in pairs for this portion of the activity.

1. Distribute sentence strips and sticky notes to students.

2. Have each student choose a sentence to copy out of their reading book and write it on one side of the sentence strip.

3. Next, ask them to copy each word in their sentence on individual sticky notes.

4. Instruct students to turn their sentence strip over so the blank side is showing and to exchange their sentence strip (blank side up) and sticky notes with their partner.

5. Have students arrange each other's sticky notes on the blank side of the sentence strip to make a good sentence.

               ↻ The partners may watch each other, taking turns to create a good sentence, so they can guide each other if necessary.

6. When they are done, tell students to check their sentence by turning over the sentence strip and looking at the original side of the sentence strip.

Stretching Students' Learning

       ◎ Increase the length and complexity of the sentences to be read and deconstructed.

       ◎ This activity can also be done by asking students to change entire phrases (subject and predicate).

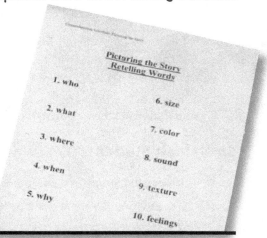

Picturing the Story

Activity Overview

Good readers make pictures in their minds as they read, which facilitates their understanding of the text. When students read without making pictures, their understanding is limited to what they can remember about the words. When students make pictures in their mind, they can then refer back to their pictures as a source of reference for comprehension as well as for recalling the words. Picturing the Story reinforces the use of pictures to deepen students' understanding of what they read. Additionally, it emphasizes the use of mental images as students formulate oral and written responses to reading.

Materials • • • • • • •

- Overhead projector and pens
- Transparency and student copies of Story Map Worksheet (see Appendix A)
- Retelling Words List (see Appendix A)
- Chart paper and marker
- Writing paper

Whole Class Instruction

Set the purpose. Say: "Making mental pictures will help you understand what you read. Picturing the Story is an activity that will give you practice using your mental pictures to retell stories both aloud and in writing."

A good way to practice making mental images with students is to use short passages at first (a good resource for these is *Visualizing and Verbalizing Stories* by Lindamood-Bell). You can create your own list of retelling words depending on your students' ability level. The Retelling Words List (see Appendix A) introduced in Thinking in Pictures and reproduced below has 10 words on it. The first five words are the basic retelling words—the *who, what, why, where,* and *when* question words. They are a good list to begin with. As students increase their retelling skill, you can increase expectations for them to structure their retells using more of the words on the list. Post a copy of the retelling words list on a wall where students can see it.

Retelling Words

1. who
2. what
3. where
4. when
5. why
6. size
7. color
8. sound
9. texture
10. feelings

1. Read a short story (it can be a one-page story, or something similar, but not too long for a beginning point, even with older students). Remind students to make mental pictures as they listen to the story.

Sample Story

Wilbur and Orville Wright: The Flying Brothers

Wilbur and Orville Wright were the first people to fly an airplane. The brothers lived in Dayton, Ohio. They built bicycles for a living. Wilbur and Orville loved to design and invent new bicycles. The brothers opened their own bike shop in 1892.

As young boys, the brothers received a flying toy from their father. They became fascinated by the idea of flying. Wilbur spent his spare time reading many books about flying. He thought human flight was possible. Soon the brothers began to build gliders as well as bicycles. Gliders are a type of plane with no engine. The Wright brothers built three gliders in all. With each new glider they learned more and more about flying. They collected data on wing design. Some of the data tables they created are still used today.

In 1903, Wilbur and Orville Wright built an airplane. This airplane was different from their gliders. This airplane had an engine to power it. They named this airplane "The Flyer."

Excerpt taken from *The Six-Minute Solution: A Reading Fluency Program* (page 118), by G. Adams and S. Brown, 2007, Longmont, CO: Sopris West Educational Services.

2. Model creating a story map on the overhead projector using a transparency of the Story Map Worksheet. Think aloud about your images as you create four sketches, showing what happened first, next, then, and finally.

☞ Ask the class to help you generate ideas for what you should put in the pictures for your story map. These pictures will give the basic sequence of the story but should also contain enough detail so that when you go back to retell the story as you look at your pictures, you will be able to find the details of who, what, where, when, size, feeling, etc., as you look at your sketches.

Story Map Worksheet

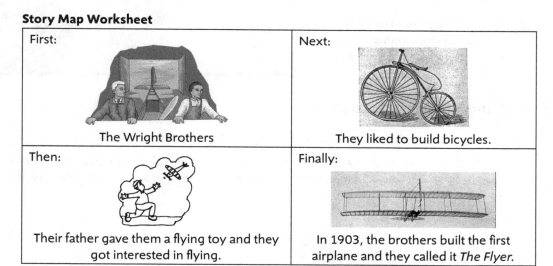

First:	Next:
The Wright Brothers	They liked to build bicycles.

Then:	Finally:
Their father gave them a flying toy and they got interested in flying.	In 1903, the brothers built the first airplane and they called it *The Flyer*.

3. After you have modeled the creation of the story map, begin your oral retelling of the story. Describe the first box of the story, and then ask the class to help you describe what happened in the rest of the sequence as you point to the box titled "Next," and so on.

Return to the purpose. Say: "Making pictures in your mind helps you understand what you read. This activity gives you practice making mental pictures to help you retell and write about what you have read."

Small Group Work

This is not primarily an art activity—the creation of quick pictures that represent images derived while reading is the focus. Drawing detailed pictures based on the text read is a valuable activity but one that should not be done during reading instruction. It can be included in a long-term project, a homework assignment, or as part of a collaborative learning activity.

1. Use a short passage again for your read-aloud. Remind students to make pictures in their mind as they listen.

2. When you are done, distribute the Story Map Worksheet and a Retelling Words List.

3. Ask the group to generate ideas about what happened first, next, then, and finally.

4. Have students draw the sequence of the story on their Story Map Worksheet, adding details from their Retelling Words List.

5. When they are finished with the drawings, ask students to share their ideas, using their images as a guide while retelling the story.

6. After everyone has retold the story, use chart paper to create a written story summary based on the group pictures and the oral retells of the students.

Independent Practice

- ⊚ Ask students to independently write a summary of the story that was read and discussed in the small group.

- ⊚ Allow students who need more support to work with another student and create a summary together.

Stretching Students' Learning

- ⊚ Increase the length and complexity of the text to be read and visualized.

- ⊚ For students who are ready for more challenge, have them take a new passage or story, read it, create images, and then write a summary of the story (see Picture Perfect Notes earlier in this section for more ideas).

Living Concept Maps

Activity Overview

Concept maps are graphic representations that help students organize their thinking to make concepts they are reading easier to understand and remember. This activity gets students up and actively engaged in the concepts that are being analyzed. Students have fun becoming a part of the concept map. They may be exposed to concept maps for years on paper and not make any deep connection with what they really represent. Creating a living concept map will help students experience how useful a graphic organizer can be in solidifying their learning.

Materials

- Card stock and marker
- Whiteboard (or chart paper), dry-erase marker, and eraser
- Index cards
- Masking tape
- Sticky notes
- Chart paper
- File folders
- Pieces of yarn
- Blank paper

Whole Classroom Instruction

Set the purpose. Say: "Using a concept map can help organize your thoughts and ideas and can make learning easier. Today you are going to create a concept map based on a story you have been reading. The concept map will help you think about and understand the story more clearly."

This activity can be done at different grade levels with both narrative and expository text. The sample story for this concept map is "Tim's Buddy"*, a decodable text:

1. Decide on three categories (e.g., main topic, themes, events) that will be included in the concept map. This step can be done with the class or you can prepare it ahead of time.

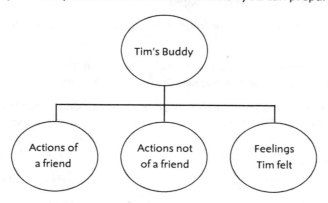

*Ebbers, Susan M. (2007.) *Power Readers* (Book 28). Longmont, CO; Sopris West Educational Services.

2. Write the categories on card stock.

3. Draw the concept map on a whiteboard and explain the categories to the class.

4. Give students index cards (the number will depend on students' level).

5. Divide the class into thirds and tell each third one of the categories to respond to.

   ☺ Have students write a response to the category on their card. For example, a response to the category "Actions of a friend."

Students bring their concept map to life!

6. Create the concept map on the floor, using the pieces of card stock with the categories written on them. Give the category cards to some of the students to hold and have them stand in the same pattern as the concept map drawn on the whiteboard.

7. Call on students one at a time to read their response and then have them stand by the person holding the appropriate category of the concept map.

   ☺ Eventually all the students will be standing by one or another part of the map, participating in the creation of the concept map.

Return to the purpose. Say: "You've been practicing creating a concept map. Concept maps can help organize your thoughts and make learning information easier—and when your classmates stand up as part of a concept map, you can see what everyone else is thinking."

Small Group Work

1. Distribute sticky notes and file folders to the group.

2. Select a main topic for another concept map, such as *Native Americans*, and draw the concept map on chart paper.

3. Ask students to think of three categories for the concept map (for instance, *culture*, *foods*, and *homes*), and add those to the chart paper.

4. Have students put sticky notes in their folder in the pattern of a concept map, following a pattern that you have modeled.

5. Ask each student, working alone, to add one sticky note to each category on their folder that the group has come up with, such as one fact about Native American culture, foods, or homes.

6. Have students share their reasons for adding the ideas they decided to add to their folders. As they share, incorporate all of their ideas on the concept map you have drawn on the chart paper.

Independent Practice

Have students work with a partner to create a concept map on a desk or on the floor.

1. Distribute index cards and yarn, and one sheet of blank paper to each pair of students.

Comprehension

2. Tell students to choose a concept that is related to a unit of study, discuss what categories they will use in their map, and then create the map by connecting cards with yarn (using tape or a stapler) on a desk or the floor.

3. When they are done creating their concept map, have the partners copy their map onto a piece of paper that can be added to a bulletin board or word wall.

Stretching Students' Learning

◉ Have students create their own concept maps as part of new learning or based on individual research they may be doing.

◉ Create different kinds of concept maps. For example, students might use a Venn diagram to compare and contrast concepts you have been studying in class.

Appendix A
✦ Worksheets ✦

1. Sound Toss Worksheet
2. Sound Box Worksheet
3. Star Cards Template
4. Star Sounds Worksheet
5. Rhyming Rhythms Worksheet
6. Word Web Worksheet
7. Speed Drill Worksheet
8. Word Chain Worksheet
9. Picture Perfect Spelling Worksheet
10. Syllable Sorting Worksheet
11. Word Line Worksheet
12. Baseball Card Worksheet
13. Word Train Worksheet
14. Branching Out Worksheet
15. Links to My Life Worksheet
16. Sentence Coding Worksheet
17. Thinking in Pictures Worksheet
18. Retelling Words List
19. Sentence Stem Worksheet
20. What's in the Bucket? Worksheet
21. Story Map Worksheet

Sound Toss Worksheet

Write the word: _____

Roll the die.

1. Write the first sound	2. Write the second sound	3. Write the third sound
4. Tap the sounds	5. Make a rhyme	6. Stretch the sounds

Sound Box Worksheet

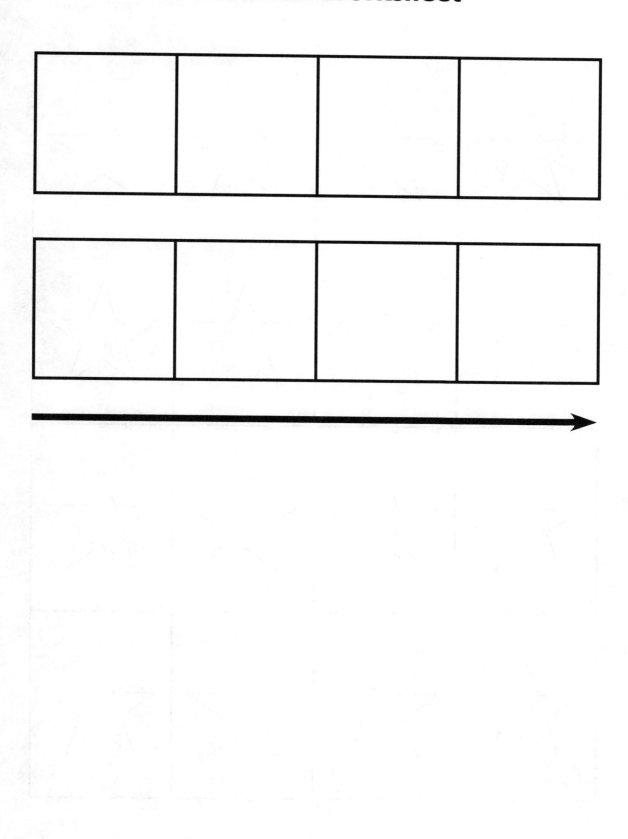

Star Cards Template

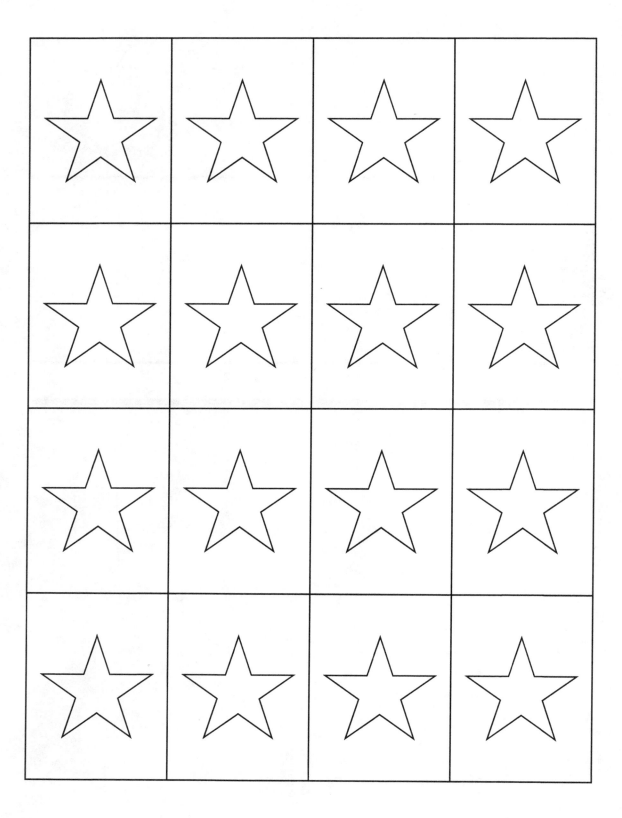

☆ Star Sounds Worksheet ☆

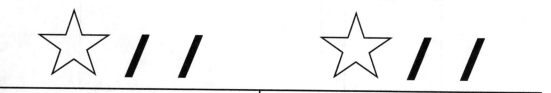

Rhyming Rhythms Worksheet

Word Web Worksheet

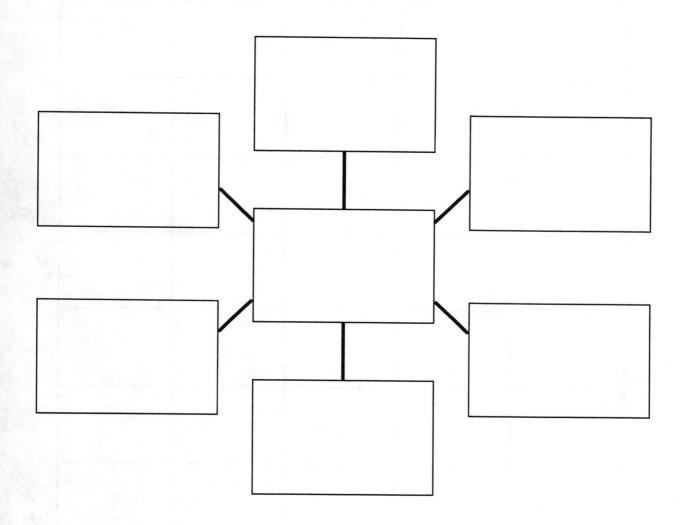

Speed Drill Worksheet

Word Chain Worksheet

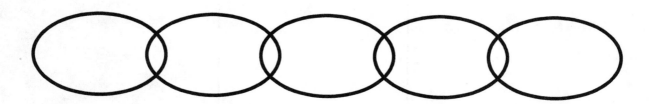

Write a sentence with one or more of the words.

❶ _____

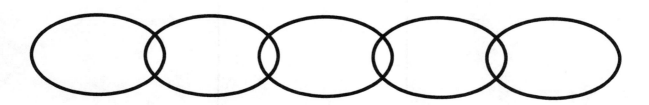

Write a sentence with one or more of the words.

❷ _____

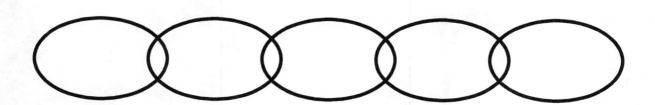

Write a sentence with one or more of the words.

❸ _____

Picture Perfect Spelling Worksheet

Word List	Write the Word in Color	Rewrite the Word

Syllable Sorting Worksheet

Closed Syllables	Open Syllables	Magic *e* Syllables

Word Line Worksheet

Sentences

Baseball Card Worksheet

Word: _____

Meaning: _____

(continued)

Use it in a sentence: _____

_____

_____

Connect it to another word: _____

Use both words in a sentence: _____

_____

_____

Do you know any other meanings? _____

_____

_____

Do you know a synonym? _____

Do you know an antonym? _____

Word Train Worksheet

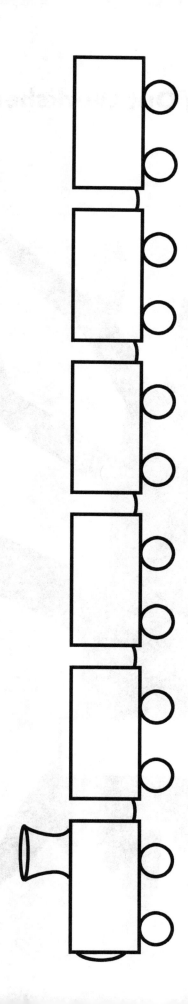

Branching Out Worksheet

Links to My Life Worksheet

Connect to:

1. your life
2. a story you have heard
3. a book you have read
4. a movie you have seen
5. your friends
6. your family
7. your community or your world

Linking what you are learning to your own life can help you learn faster and remember better so that when you want to use your new learning, you can!

Sentence Coding Worksheet

Students can code for any part of sentence grammar that has been taught directly, such as: subject and predicate, adjectives, adverbs.

Example:

Subject: who, what	Code with a box around it	The little girl runs quickly.
Predicate: is doing	Code by underlining	The little girl <u>runs quickly</u>.
Adjective: describes the noun	Code with a circle	The (little) girl runs quickly.
Adverb: describes the verb	Code with a wavy line	The little girl runs quickly.

Copy the sentence you are working with:

_____

Now You Try It!

Subject: who, what	Box	
Predicate: is doing	Underline	
Adjective: describes the noun	Circle	
Adverb: describes the verb	Wavy line	

Thinking in Pictures Worksheet

Text Name: _____

Word, Idea, or Character	Visualize It

Retelling Words List

1. who   6. size

2. what   7. color

3. where   8. sound

4. when   9. texture

5. why   10. feelings

Sentence Stem Worksheet

Write your sentence:

_____

_____

_____

What's In the Bucket? Worksheet

Write your sentence:

_____

_____

_____

Story Map Worksheet

First:

_____

_____

_____

Next:

_____

_____

_____

Then:

_____

_____

_____

Finally:

_____

_____

_____

Appendix B
Letter Cards

From Lacey, K., & Baird, W. (2005.) *WatchWord: A multisensory reading and writing program.* Longmont, CO: Sopris West Educational Services.

T	t
A	a
S	s

M m

P p

C c

O o

N n

D d

G g

l i

B b

F   f

Z   z

K   k

H h

U u

V v

L

I

J

j

Y

y

R r

E e

W w

X x

Qu qu

Digraph

Digraph

sh ch

192

Digraph

th

Consonant Combination

wh

Digraph

ck

Double Vowel

ee

Double Vowel

ea

Double Vowel

ai

Double Vowel

Double Vowel

ay

oa

Double Vowel

Double Vowel

ow

oe

Double Vowel

Double Vowel

ew

ue

oo

ie

ye

igh

Bibliography

Adams, G., & Brown, S. (2007). *The six-minute solution: A reading fluency program.* (2007). Longmont, CO: Sopris West Educational Services.

Adams, M. (1990). *Beginning to read: Thinking and learning about print.* Cambridge, MA: MIT Press.

Beck, I. L., McKeown, M. G., & Kucan, L. (2002). *Bringing words to life: Robust vocabulary instruction.* New York: Guilford Press.

Beck, I. L., McKeown, M. G., & Kucan, L. (Eds.) (1997). *Questioning the author: An approach for enhancing student engagement with text.* Newark: DE: International Reading Association.

Beck. R., Conrad D., & Anderson, P. (1997). *Basic skill builders.* Longmont, CO: Sopris West Educational Services.

Ebbers, S. M. (2007). *Power readers.* Longmont, CO: Sopris West Educational Services.

Ebbers, S. M. (2004). *Vocabulary through morphemes.* Longmont, CO: Sopris West Educational Services.

Foorman, B., Fletcher, J., & Francis, D. (1997). *A scientific approach to reading instruction.* Learning Disabilities Online. Available at: http://www.ldonline.org/ld_indepth/reading/cars.html

Good, R. H. III, & Kaminski, R. (2003). *DIBELS: Dynamic indicators of basic early literacy skills.* Longmont, CO: Sopris West Educational Services.

Hammill, D. D., Wiederholt, J. L., & Allen, E. A. (2006). *Test of silent contextual reading fluency* (TOSCRF). Austin, TX: Pro-Ed.

Henry, M. (2003). *Unlocking literacy: Effective decoding and spelling instruction.* Baltimore: Paul Brookes Publishing.

Hudson, R. F., Mercer, C. D., & Lane, H. B. (2000). *Exploring reading fluency: A paradigmatic overview.* Unpublished manuscript, University of Florida, Gainesville.

Mather, N., Hammill, D. D., Allen, E. A., & Roberts, R. (2004). *Test of silent word reading fluency.* (TOSWRF). Austin, TX: Pro-Ed.

Mathes, P. G., Allor, H. J., Torgesen, J. K., & Allen, S. H. (2001). *Teacher-Directed PALS.* Longmont, CO: Sopris West Educational Services.

Moats, L. C. (2005). *Language essentials for teachers of reading and spelling (LETRS).* Longmont, CO: Sopris West Educational Services. Modules 1-12.

Moats, L. C. (2000). *Speech to print: Language essentials for teachers.* Baltimore, MD: Paul H. Brookes Publishing.

National Reading Panel. (2000). *Report of the National Reading Panel: Teaching children to read: An evidence-based assessment of the scientific research literature on reading and its implications for reading instruction*. Washington, DC: U.S. Government Printing Office.

Shaywitz, S. E. (2003). *Overcoming dyslexia. A new and complete science-based program for reading problems at any level*. New York: Alfred A. Knopf.

Snow, C. E., Burns M. S., & Griffin, P. (1998). *Preventing reading difficulties in young children*. Washington, DC: National Academy Press.

Torgesen, J. K., Wagner, R. K., & Rashotte, C. A. (1999). *Test of word reading efficiency* (TOWRE). Austin, TX: Pro-Ed.

Wolf, M. (2001). *Dyslexia, fluency, and the brain*. Baltimore, MD: York Press.

Wolfe, P., & Nevills, P. (2004). *Building the reading brain*. Thousand Oakes, CA. Corwin Press.

Glossary

automaticity performance without conscious effort or attention; a characteristic of skill mastery

affix a meaningful part of a word attached before or after a root to modify its meaning

alphabetic principle the principle that letters are used to represent individual phonemes in the spoken word; a critical insight for beginning reading and spelling

alphabetic writing system a system of symbols that represent each consonant and vowel sound in a language

base word a free morpheme to which affixes can be added

chunk a group of letters, processed as a unit, that corresponds to a piece of a word, usually a consonant cluster, rime pattern, syllable, or morpheme

closed syllable a written syllable containing a single vowel letter that ends in one or more consonants; the vowel sound is short

consonant a phoneme (speech sound) that is not a vowel and that is formed by obstructing the flow of air with the teeth, lips, or tongue; English has 25 consonant phonemes

consonant blend adjacent consonants that appear before or after a vowel

consonant digraph a two-letter combination that represents one speech sound that is not represented by either letter alone (e.g., **sh**, **th**, **wh**)

consonant-le syllable a written syllable found at the ends of words such as dawdle, single, and rubble

cognitive desktop a figurative expression referring to the working memory capacity of the mind and the available attentional resources in consciousness

concept an idea that links facts, words, and ideas together as a coherent whole

context the language that surrounds a given word or phrase (linguistic context), or the field of meaningful associations that surrounds a given word or phrase (experiential context)

context processor the neural networks that bring background knowledge and discourse to bear as word meanings are processed

cumulative instruction teaching that proceeds in additive steps, building on what has previously been taught

decodable text text in which a high proportion of words (80%–90%) comprise sound-symbol relationships that have already been taught; used to provide practice with specific decoding skills; a bridge between learning phonics and the application of phonics in independent reading of text

decoding the ability to translate a word from print to speech, usually by employing knowledge of sound-symbol correspondences; also the act of deciphering a new word by sounding it out

dialects mutually intelligible versions of the same language with systematic differences in phonology, word use, and/or grammatical rules

digraph (see consonant digraph)

direct instruction the teacher defines and teaches a concept, guides children through its application, and arranges for extended guided practice until mastery is achieved

dyslexia an impairment of reading accuracy and fluency attributable to an underlying phonological processing problem

ELL English language learner

encoding producing written symbols for spoken language; also spelling by sounding out

explicit instruction instruction wherein the teacher defines the concept or association the student is to learn, provides guided practice with feedback, provides additional independent practice, and checks to see if the concept was learned, retained, and applied

expository text factual text written to "put out" information

grapheme a letter or letter combination that spells a phoneme; can be one, two, three, or four letters in English (e.g., **e**, **ei**, **igh**, **eigh**)

indirect vocabulary learning the process of learning words through incidental and contextual exposures, rather than through direct and deliberate teaching

integrated when lesson components are interwoven and flow smoothly together

long-term memory the memory system that stores information beyond 24-hours

Matthew Effect coined by Keith Stanovich; a reference to the Biblical passage that the "rich get richer and the poor get poorer," insofar as the pattern of language and reading skills development in individuals over time

meaning processor the neural networks that attach meanings to words that have been heard or decoded

meta-cognition the ability to reflect on and understand our own thought processes

meta-linguistic awareness an acquired level of awareness of language structure and function that allows us to reflect on and consciously manipulate the language we use

morpheme the smallest meaningful unit of language

morphology the study of the meaningful units in the language and how they are combined in word formation

morphophonemic having to do with both sound and meaning

multisyllabic having more than one syllable

narrative text that tells about sequences of events, usually with the structure of a story, fiction or nonfiction; often contrasted with expository text that reports factual information and the relationships among ideas

orthographic processor the neural networks responsible for perceiving, storing, and retrieving the letter sequences in words

orthography a writing system for representing language

paraphrase express the thoughts in a sentence with different words

phoneme a speech sound that combines with others in a language system to make words

phoneme awareness (also phonemic awareness) the conscious awareness that words are made up of segments of our own speech that are represented with letters in an alphabetic orthography

phonics the study of the relationships between letters and the sounds they represent; also used as a descriptor for code-based instruction in reading (e.g., "the phonics approach" or "phonic reading")

phonological awareness meta-linguistic awareness of all levels of the speech sound system, including word boundaries, stress patterns, syllables, onset-rime units, and phonemes; a more encompassing term than phoneme awareness

phonological processor a neural network in the frontal and temporal areas of the brain, usually the left cerebral hemisphere, that is specialized for speech sound perception and memory

phonological working memory the "on-line" memory system that holds speech in mind long enough to extract meaning from it, or that holds onto words during reading and writing; a function of the phonological processor

phonology the rule system within a language by which phonemes can be sequenced and uttered to make words

phrase-cued reading the act of reading phrases that have already been marked or designated by underlining, spacing, or arrangement on the page

prefix a morpheme that precedes a root and that contributes to or modifies the meaning of a word; a common linguistic unit in Latin-based words

reading fluency the ability to read text with sufficient speed and accuracy to support deep comprehension

root a bound morpheme, usually of Latin origin, that cannot stand alone but that is used to form a family of words with related meanings

scaffolding providing extra structure or support that enables the learner to perform successfully

schwa the "empty" vowel in an unaccented syllable, such as the last syllables of *circus* and *bagel*

semantics the study of word and phrase meanings

shallow word learning partial or limited knowledge of a word that may be constricted to one context or one meaning instead of several

sound-symbol correspondence same as phoneme-grapheme correspondence; the rules and patterns by which letters and letter combinations represent speech sounds

structural analysis the study of affixes, base words, and roots

suffix a derivational morpheme added to a root or base that often changes the word's part of speech and that modifies its meaning

syllable the unit of pronunciation that is organized around a vowel, it may or may not have consonants before or after the vowel

syllabic consonants /m/, /n/, /l/, and /r/ can do the job of a vowel and make an unaccented syllable at the ends of words such as rhythm, mitten, little, and letter

syntax the rule system by which words can be ordered in sentences

vocabulary the body of words known by the speaker of a language, receptive or listening vocabulary is the body of word meanings recognized in context, whereas expressive vocabulary is the body of word meanings known well enough that they can be used appropriately by the speaker of a language

vowel one of a set of 15 vowel phonemes in English, not including vowel-r combinations; an open phoneme that is the nucleus of every syllable; classified by tongue position and height (high-low, front-back)

word recognition the instant recognition of a whole word in print